WHY
DEALS
FAIL

ANNA FAELTEN is a corporate finance adviser at EY (Ernst & Young), an international accountancy and professional-services firm. She has ten years of experience in mergers and acquisitions (M&A), predominantly advising firms in the technology, media and telecommunications sector. She is a visiting lecturer at Cass Business School, where she teaches M&A to master's degree students. She remains active with her academic research, which focuses on M&A but also encompasses general corporate finance, corporate governance, corporate distress, and restructuring and investment in emerging markets.

MICHEL DRIESSEN is a senior partner within the transaction advisory services practice at EY. He has previously held senior executive positions at Accenture, Visa and Rabobank. During his nine years at EY he has worked on and led over 100 multibillion-pound transactions with the world's largest corporates and private equity firms on some of the biggest and most complex cross-border engagements. His focus has been on synergy identification and valuation, post-merger integration, divestments/carve-outs and operational restructuring. He is an advisory board member of the M&A Research Centre and a senior visiting fellow at Cass Business School.

SCOTT MOELLER is a professor in the practice of finance at Cass Business School, where he is also director of the M&A Research Centre. He is a former investment banker at both Morgan Stanley and Deutsche Bank, a former consultant at Booz Allen Hamilton, co-author of *Intelligent M&A: Navigating the Mergers and Acquisitions Minefield* (now in its second edition), author of *Surviving M&A: Make the Most of Your Company Being Acquired*, and editor of *Finance Essentials: The Practitioners' Guide* and *M&A Collection: Themes in Best Practice*.

WHY DEALS FAIL

AND HOW TO RESCUE THEM

M&A lessons for business success

**Anna Faelten, Michel Driessen
and Scott Moeller**

The Economist Books

PublicAffairs
New York

The Economist in Association with Profile Books Ltd. and PublicAffairs

Copyright © Anna Faelten, Michel Driessen and Scott Moeller, 2016.

First published in 2016 by Profile Books Ltd. in Great Britain.

Published in 2016 in the United States by PublicAffairs™,
an imprint of Perseus Books, LLC, a subsidiary of Hachette Book Group, Inc.

PublicAffairs books are available at special discounts for bulk purchases in the U.S. by corporations, institutions, and other organizations. For more information, please contact the Special Markets Department at the Perseus Books Group, 2300 Chestnut Street, Suite 200, Philadelphia, PA 19103, call (800) 810-4145, ext. 5000, or e-mail special.markets@perseusbooks.com.

Typeset in Milo by MacGuru Ltd
info@macguru.org.uk

Library of Congress Control Number: 2016945398
ISBN 978-1-61039-790-2 (PB)
ISBN 978-1-61039-791-9 (EB)

First Edition

10 9 8 7 6 5 4 3 2 1

To Mattias, with all my love
AF

To Celine, Edsard and Jasper, the pride in my life
MD

To Daniela, Christine, Andrew, Ellen and Jonathan, with love
SM

Contents

Figures and tables

Figures

Tables

Preface

IF THE GLOBAL ECONOMY had a characteristic sound when this book was being written, it was champagne corks popping in the offices of merger & acquisition (M&A) advisers from London to Shanghai and New York. Global dealmaking escaped its austerity shackles, breaking the $5 trillion barrier in 2015 and easily eclipsing the $3.7 trillion record set in 2007, according to data on announced deals compiled by Dealogic.

Whether future years match or even exceed those levels again, M&A will remain a catalyst for business transformation worldwide – even when the economic cycle inevitably turns downward again. Examined through the lens of history, more deals were done in 2009, a trough following the last recession, than in almost any prior peak year. M&A deals have become an accepted driver of business growth and boards use those deals as a tool to achieve corporate expansion, whether into new products and geographic markets or to consolidate with a current or potential competitor. The headline sums involved over the past 35 years are staggering. Looking at the global picture, the combined value of all M&A deals from 1980 to the end of 2015 (almost $65 trillion) is bigger than the current annual world economy value outside the US. In that same period, almost 900,000 deals were announced.

Many were questionable or poorly executed, as we will show in this book. With companies expected to continue to merge in record numbers, it is time to learn some critical lessons from those deals.

So, M&A is an increasingly important feature of the global economy, but does dealmaking hurt or help business and the economy overall? The answer is that M&A, when properly done, drives corporate and economic growth, thus creating jobs and fostering innovations, among other benefits. The inverse, however, is also true: M&A, badly done, can damage business and, by extension, the economy and result in hundreds if not thousands of employees being made redundant.

In 2014 the government of the UK – one of the most active markets globally for M&A – commissioned Cass Business School's Mergers and Acquisitions Research Centre (MARC) to investigate whether M&A has a negative or positive impact on the country's economy.

To answer this question, MARC conducted research on UK-listed entities, measuring the short-term or direct impact of the deals made in the period 1997 to 2007 – the share-price reaction on the day the deal was announced – and the longer-term impact measured by share-price development and financial performance in the two to three years after the transaction. The answer was that M&A deals do generate short-term benefits for the economy, especially because some large deals were spectacularly successful. However, over the longer term, the results are less clear. Despite some highly successful tie-ups that drove the economic results to an overall positive average, the majority of UK acquisitions by number in the research period actually destroyed value. In summary, deals can be hugely beneficial for all involved when you get it right, but they still struggle to live up to their initial hype – and potential.

The solution is to get the deal strategy and execution right – and in this book we will show you how. *Why Deals Fail* is aimed at business people who want to understand better how M&A can drive corporate fortunes. Whether you are a seasoned M&A professional, an employee in a company that is acquiring or being acquired, or a newly graduated business student wanting to know more about dealmaking, this book will help you to make the right decisions when they are most crucial.

Most of the deals detailed in this book are lessons in what not to do; we will lift the corporate veil to show you what went wrong when huge and otherwise highly successful global businesses such as Royal Bank of Scotland (RBS), Microsoft and HP embarked on M&A transactions. But we will also show you large and small companies that got it right, such as Diageo and Centrica. Thus some case studies are examples of why deals fail, whereas others take the opposite view on how to rescue them.

Chapter by chapter, we take you through each stage of a takeover process, ending each one with a simple set of guidelines – a "dos and don'ts" list – to keep deals on track. There are lessons from small family-owned businesses, such as Timpson, a shoe-repair and key-cutting firm, that large companies should emulate, and conversely lessons from some large companies that can be used by small and medium-sized businesses.

Part 1: Pre-deal

Chapter 1 discusses the starting point to any transaction, namely the need to align the M&A strategy with the overarching corporate strategy. There are several alternatives to M&A – or corporate status if you will – all of which should be carefully considered before embarking on the arguably riskiest option, that is, a full corporate M&A deal.

Main case studies – Chapter 1

French food company Danone and China's Wahaha; law firm Wachtell, Lipton, Rosen & Katz.

Once managers have decided to use M&A to achieve their aims, a carefully devised target-selection process is crucial for success, in terms of securing the deal and also to establish that the selected target is indeed fit for strategic purpose. This is the subject of Chapter 2.

Main case studies – Chapter 2

Global spirits producer Diageo's pursuit of three emerging-market targets; the banking merger between RBS and ABN AMRO; Timpson's acquisition of Max Spielmann.

Chapter 3 addresses the first phase of the all-important due diligence process. It looks at the pitfalls and risks of cutting corners at this stage of the process, covering both the traditional tangible due diligence areas such as financials, IT, legal and operations, and crucial intangible aspects such as people, culture and ethics.

Main case studies – Chapter 3

Carmakers BMW and Volkswagen in their pursuit of Rolls-Royce; the proposed merger between soft drinks producers Britvic and A. G. Barr.

The issue of value versus price is critical in dealmaking. Chapter 4 outlines the steps needed to establish the buyer's walkaway price (value) and the seller's, or market's, view on value (price).

Main case studies – Chapter 4

Vista Equity Partner's takeover of financial-technology provider Misys; Rio Tinto's acquisition of Alcan.

Part 2: The deal

There are as many negotiating tactics as there are deals, but the overriding theme is that knowledge is power. Chapter 5 discusses ways in which companies and their advisers can use the knowledge and expertise developed in the first four chapters to the best advantage. It considers the various types of corporate scenarios from auctions to hostile bids. It profiles a legendary investment banker, Bruce Wasserstein, and looks at what takes place during a deal at the first meeting between the two chief executives.

Main case studies – Chapter 5

The foreign purchase of Manchester United; the failure of one of the world's largest companies, Microsoft, to buy Yahoo!; pharmaceutical company Shire's agreed takeover of Baxalta.

A high-quality communication plan is crucial to the success of a deal; this can be done in-house or by external public relations (PR) advisers. Chapter 6 assesses the benefits of PR advice and provides insight from two PR professionals. It also looks at the growing importance of activist investors.

Main case studies – Chapter 6

Insurance company Prudential's failed bid for AIA.

Regulators are a growing challenge to dealmakers, especially in larger deals and cross-border M&A. Chapter 7 guides you through the world's biggest regulators, such as the European Commission's Competition Division, and introduces you to national governments and their agendas on foreign investment. This necessarily includes local rules relating to "proper behaviour" during a takeover.

Main case studies – Chapter 7

Global food group Kraft's takeover of the UK-based confectioner Cadbury; the blocked merger between two of the largest stock exchanges in the world, NYSE Euronext and Deutsche Börse; the failure of Dubai Ports World, based in the United Arab Emirates, to include US ports in its acquisition of P&O.

Part 3: Post-deal

The earlier parts of this book are mostly about doing the right deal. Chapter 8 looks at how to do a deal the right way. This is fundamentally about good integration planning and execution. Done properly, integration starts at the deal-planning phase as discussed in part 1 and 2, and really kicks in after the deal is announced. At that point, if executed well, you will see the structure of the merged company put in place and integration already beginning. If the process looks challenging at this point, it may be because the deal was ill conceived – and deals can fall apart in this phase. The second part of the chapter considers post-closing integration, and in particular the first 100 days.

Main case studies – Chapter 8

The abandoned merger of two leading public relations companies, Omnicom and Publicis; Action for Blind People's merger with the Royal National Institute of Blind People; mobile-phone company Zain's African expansion; energy and services company Centrica's integration of Venture Productions.

What happens when a merger fails? History tells us that corporate marriages do not always last forever; even a deal that appears now to be very right may not be so in ten years' time, particularly as the world economy or new technologies develop in ways that dramatically change markets. A split – or corporate divorce – need not be a bad thing: as Chapter 9 shows, divisions that were unloved by their large corporate owners can go on to be a huge success with different backers or even as independent companies. However, once a split does become inevitable, special attention is needed over issues such as staff and governance to ensure an amicable break-up.

Main case studies – Chapter 9

The demerger of one of the largest-ever tech deals (the merger of HP and Compaq); BC Partners' purchase of Mergermarket Group from publisher Pearson.

The concluding chapter ends with a challenge to readers to keep the learning current on how to make deals even better.

*

This book originated as an idea that Anna Faelten and Scott Moeller had while working at Cass Business School. Many books on "how to do deals" exist and some document deals that failed. But there did not seem to be any that linked the two. Thus began the planning for a book that looked at big and small failures but went several steps further, identifying not just why they failed but what could have been done to avoid those failures, thus providing guidance for future deals. When Anna later moved to start working at EY she discussed the book with Michel Driessen, and he joined the authorship team to share insights from his experience in this area.

Together, we discussed the issue of why deals fail. Surprisingly, we quickly came to a joint conclusion that, among the dozens of reasons provided in many textbooks and articles on the topic, there are three that stand out: planning, communication and people. These are outlined in the Introduction and are referred to throughout the book.

We hope that this book provides a practical guide and insight to managers and other interested readers on the dos and don'ts of making a deal a success. As you will see, a successful deal is not easy to achieve, and it depends on the people and parties involved and a relentless focus on the three components that make a deal work.

No deal is the same as the last or the next, which is of course what makes it so fascinating, but some themes are consistent across types, sizes and geographies. We strongly believe many failures can be avoided if company executives keep track of the three big mistakes of dealmaking: planning, communication and people.

A note on terminology

There are numerous words describing dealmaking, such as transaction, acquisition, takeover, investment, deal and merger. The most important distinction is arguably between a merger and an acquisition. The technical definition of the difference – as it happens a non-standardised and debated one – is outside the scope of this book.

That said, in general, a merger is a combination of two similarly sized, often large, leading companies in the same industry that creates a new, larger company; whereas an acquisition is typically a bigger company buying out the shareholders of a smaller one, then integrating it within its own structure. Many people use these terms interchangeably, but we have tried to be careful in making the above distinctions between mergers and acquisitions.

September 2016

Introduction: The three big mistakes of dealmaking

WHEN SILICON VALLEY heavyweight Hewlett-Packard (HP) sealed a takeover of the UK's Autonomy in 2011, no one predicted the corporate car crash that would follow.

There had been few significant deals since the 2008 global financial collapse and economic slowdown, which helped HP's chief executive, Léo Apotheker, secure a reasonably upbeat reception when he made his bold statement to transform the sleepy information technology (IT) company into "a leader in the evolving information economy".

But just 12 months later, HP had lost its reputation and its chief executive and was facing write-downs of $8.8 billion, nearly 80% of the $11 billion it paid for Autonomy. Worse, in 2012, HP alleged that it had been the victim of fraud by Autonomy's management and its auditors, blaming the losses on "serious accounting improprieties, disclosure failures, and outright misrepresentations".

Autonomy and its founders have, as you would expect, publicly and categorically rejected such claims. HP, however, has agreed to pay one of its shareholders, PGGM Vermogensbeheer, a Dutch pension fund, $100 million in damages, without admitting any liability.

The company was and is facing years of legal battles. Irrespective of their outcome, the takeover will go down in history as a spectacular failure.

High expectations

Founded in a garage in Palo Alto in 1939, HP was one of the original core Silicon Valley start-ups and later the world's largest manufacturer of computers. But as the industry developed, the company found itself

FIGURE INTRO.1 **HP's share price** February 2009–December 2013

Sources: Authors; S&P CapIQ data

stuck in the low-margin business of computer hardware production, and despite its hefty $95 billion market capitalisation, its share price was suffering (see Figure Intro.1).

Under pressure from investors to improve its strategic positioning, the company brought in Apotheker as CEO in November 2010, with the strong expectation of immediate acquisitions. Apotheker was an experienced executive in the computer industry, having spent more than 20 years at SAP, a multinational German software company, and serving as co-CEO just before his appointment at HP.

A tie-up with Autonomy, a British entrepreneurial success story, looked like the solution to faster and more innovative future growth. The company, a Cambridge University spin-off, was founded in 1996. By the time of HP's bid, Autonomy was one of the FTSE 100. On August 18th 2011, HP announced a formal offer of £25.50 ($42.11) per share, a 64% premium on the previous day's closing price.

Headed by Mike Lynch, a Cambridge University engineer who started out building the technology behind music synthesisers, Autonomy was one of the fastest-growing and most dynamic software businesses in the world. Its main product, the IDOL (Intelligent Data

Operating Layer) platform, was ground-breaking and is still marketed by HP as a highly intelligent tool for indexing unstructured data.

In the year of the deal, Autonomy posted record quarterly revenues of $256 million. However, some analysts questioned not only the value of Autonomy's technology but also its accounting methods.

Richard Windsor, formerly at Nomura Securities, commented on HP's challenges to Autonomy's accounting practices:

> Autonomy's detractors have been writing about this for years and there has been the occasional obvious sign that things were not quite right. The most common red flag was that cash flow in some quarters often did not match profit. This is quite unusual in a software company.
>
> It is certainly noteworthy that HP acquired Autonomy at a record price tag, only to write down most of the price paid less than two years later, blaming the huge write off on the very accounting practices which industry experts and analysts had been questioning for years.

Whatever the legitimacy of these accounting practices, any such issues should have been dealt with at the all-important due diligence stages – both pre-announcement and pre-completion – which are covered in Chapters 3 and 8.

The transaction and its aftermath

On the day of the announcement Apotheker proudly told investors:

> HP is taking bold, transformative steps to position the company as a leader in the evolving information economy. Today's announced plan will allow HP to drive creation of long-term shareholder value.

The decision to buy your way onto a new strategic path is common practice, but there are a number of alternatives to outright M&A – outlined in detail in Chapter 1 – which perhaps would have been better and less risky for HP. Deciding on the right target company to acquire to reach your strategic aim is also tricky. Chapter 2 highlights the need to have a "live" target list where you track your most desired assets closely. Sealing a deal means finding a company that is both the right strategic fit and potentially "in play" – that is, where a deal with the existing shareholders is possible. It is possible that HP suffered from a fixation on its target (Autonomy), a common error for buyers, which means it had already lost a significant amount of bargaining power when negotiating the final price paid.

Although HP's share price rose by 15% in the wake of the announcement, reflecting an initially positive reaction by the investment community, it closed the day as the US market's worst performer. The new strategy, as laid out by management, was apparently not credible to HP's shareholders when they analysed it.

Analysts and investors challenged the ability of HP to integrate the combined business – perhaps remembering HP's problems with its 2001 merger with Compaq – and the company faced an uphill battle to convince its various stakeholders that this large bet was a good one. As demonstrated in Chapter 6, effective communication on the day of the deal's announcement is crucial, as it is management's chance to position the strategy and value behind the deal and to align the views of internal stakeholders (who have known about the deal perhaps for several months) and external stakeholders (who only find out about the deal from the public announcement).

Things quickly went from bad to worse for HP. Just weeks later, Apotheker was fired and replaced by Meg Whitman, previously CEO of eBay. Then in May 2012, after a mere eight months at HP, Lynch – who was a crucial part of the Autonomy takeover – left, taking much of Autonomy's remaining management team with him.

Many cited a culture clash between the corporate bureaucracy of HP and the more entrepreneurial, flat-structured Autonomy. As discussed throughout this book, a failure to recognise cultural differences between the buyer and the target – effectively choosing to ignore the human component of any deal – is one of the most cited reasons for M&A failure.

These days – but also at the time of the HP/Autonomy deal – the due diligence process done properly includes a comprehensive segment on culture. The importance of that cultural fit is highlighted in Chapter 3, demonstrating that cultural compatibility or potential differences must be raised early in the deal conception phase, ideally well before any public announcements and especially if people are a key component of profitability, as was the case with Autonomy.

The departure of Lynch and his team was the opening sequence of a long blame game leading, as mentioned earlier, to the now infamous $8.8 billion write-down announcement in November 2012.

Responding to allegations of fraud, Lynch replied in an open letter:

As we have said before, we believe the problem with the Autonomy acquisition by HP lies in the mismanagement of that business by HP under its ownership, making it impossible for Autonomy to deliver on HP's expectations. Autonomy's accounts were fully audited by Deloitte throughout the period in question and Deloitte has confirmed that it conducted its audit work in full compliance with regulation and professional standards. We refuse to be a scapegoat for HP's own failings.

Sadly, the HP and Autonomy story is far from unique. RBS's acquisition, together with Fortis and Banco Santander, of ABN AMRO also crosses the line between the merely misguided and downright disastrous.

In this book, these and many other examples of famous global companies and smaller, less well-known firms will demonstrate how much value has been destroyed by ill-considered or poorly executed M&A deals – and how this could have been avoided. There are a number of errors – or a common and recurring set of mistakes – which dealmakers appear to make consistently. Throughout the chapters of this book, these are summarised in a list of tips and guidelines, intended to help buyers and sellers avoid the usual pitfalls and therefore preserve value throughout the deal process.

Our assessment of these deals is, by necessity, an analysis of their impact only in the broad period following the deals. For example, following the UK government's inevitable re-flotation of RBS, the bank it bailed out during the 2008 financial crisis, it is conceivable – if unlikely – that events as yet unknown could propel RBS to the top of global banking's profitability league in, say, 15–20 years' time after the deal with ABN AMRO. But should that happen, none of the credit would belong to the men and women who executed the deal in 2007.

Introducing the big three

There were several manifest failures in the HP/Autonomy deal, as there are in many of the deals discussed in this book. These have been distilled to three overarching issues: failure of planning, failure of communication, and failure to properly consider the impact of people. These, we believe, are the three big mistakes of dealmaking:

1 Planning

The supposedly transformational acquisition of Autonomy was by its nature inherently risky, even for HP, a company valued at nearly $100 billion. The cost of Autonomy was sizeable at $11 billion. Its importance for HP was magnified because the company was pinning its future on the transaction to deliver strategic wins in terms of culture change in the core business as well as cross-selling and its own market position.

If you do not have a clear, detailed, well-thought-out and articulated deal strategy, no planning for its integration will be sufficient, as the two are inherently linked. As shown in Chapter 7, planning also entails being prepared for any pushback from the regulators, an increasingly important issue for corporate dealmakers because of the rise in cross-border acquisitions globally, among other factors.

Although large, transformational deals are not automatically destined for failure, perhaps a more gradual shift towards high-end software products, buying smaller, more easily digestible targets, would have worked better for HP. As discussed in Chapter 1, hubris is one of the most common M&A pitfalls for business leaders who are prone either to overestimate their own ability or to underestimate the scale of the task.

2 Communication

HP's failure to communicate convincingly the benefits of the deal to its shareholders, as demonstrated by the significant fall in share price on the day of the announcement, was the start of the transaction's downfall.

Effective communication is often a reflection of a well-prepared and well-aligned combined management team. The case for synergies should be clearly articulated in the due diligence phase, and the 100-day integration plan should be written by the time the deal is announced.

Knowing that in any deal there are significant risks, it was certainly appropriate for investors and analysts, for example, to ask questions about the price HP paid for Autonomy.

The deal did, as stated, represent a significant premium on Autonomy's share price, implying that HP expected to generate synergies from the deal worth, as suggested by several analysts at the time, a minimum of $2.9 billion on a net present value basis. Add to that the fact that HP was paying 24 times the trailing earnings before interest, tax and depreciation (EBITDA), and most analysts would say that the price was a stretch. And this figure did not include costs associated with the transaction such as adviser fees and integration costs, which were likely to be at least another 15–20% of the deal's price.

HP saw the transaction as the facilitator of a significant strategic shift towards high-end software and, indeed, as a tool to change the culture of its traditional core business. But when a buyer is attracted to a target because of its culture, an understanding of the specific components that make this culture unique is pivotal to making the deal work. HP might have admired Autonomy's culture, but it did not truly understand it or know how, or even whether, it could be adopted by HP's other divisions.

3 People

Poor communication and a lack of understanding of the culture of Autonomy led to the third failure: to appreciate, evaluate and consider the value of people. Autonomy's culture was what HP said it wanted, yet it failed to lock in and learn from its expensively acquired new management team and its different, more entrepreneurial culture.

In summary, HP failed in all three areas, even though a failure in just one of the big three could have been sufficient to make the deal fail overall. Generally speaking it is necessary to be successful in all three, but certain deals may require a focus in one area more than another.

The significant difference between valuation and pricing in M&A is discussed in Chapter 4, but the high price paid in this case implied that HP knowingly paid a premium over Autonomy's pre-deal market valuation. HP must have seen real strategic business value in Autonomy as well as in its culture and management team, aspects that are difficult to assign a financial value to. It would have also assumed significant post-deal synergies, helping to justify the price paid. In hindsight, it is clear that those synergies were overstated or the estimated risk of delivering the same was understated.

As Autonomy's management team pointed out following HP's court filing disclosures in September 2014, HP's own estimated revenue synergies of $7.4 billion as a result of the two businesses operating as a combined entity was certainly a hefty target and, they claimed, the real reason behind the significant write-down. In its own court filings, HP pushed the argument of misstated underlying revenues which had led it to believe Autonomy had more potential – and value to HP – than was actually the case. The correct valuation is the result of sound and achievable financial forecasts based on accurate and well-researched due diligence data, none of which appeared to have been present in this particular deal.

Although price and value are referred to here, they are not categorised as being among the big three mistakes.

Pricing is a significant potential concern, but we do not believe that mispricing is generally terminal. First, there is no such thing as "one right price" in an M&A context. What the buyer ultimately pays for the target is based on its own views regarding the financial future value of the target, including the potential synergies as a result of the two businesses combining and any changes that the buyer may make post-deal. Clearly, the inputs into a financial model to determine the value will be different from bidder to bidder, and these are ultimately different from the view of the seller, who sees its company on a stand-alone basis. The difference here is what creates the opportunity to transact a deal, so the price paid will be incorrect for anyone but the buyer that closes the deal. The highest bidder will usually – but not always – prevail, and even though a full price was paid, it can be deemed a success if the underlying predictions are correct.

Second, determining whether the price paid was "right" can only be done with the benefit of hindsight. There are a plethora of other factors that can destroy value for the acquirer. We have seen many deals where the pricing was certainly considered as full and the buyer was able to achieve its aims despite this. Mispricing in this context – where a price is paid well above market expectations – is the one major error that companies can recover from. However, appropriate pricing, meaning not overpaying, does make success easier to achieve.

Few M&A transactions collapse as dramatically as HP's takeover of Autonomy, but a far greater proportion fall far short of their promise to deliver on the expected value creation.

Numerous studies from the 1980s and 1990s show a failure rate as high as 70–80%. But it is getting better. The best-case scenario in more recent studies is a success rate of just under 50%. Given the opportunities for value destruction of such a significant corporate event, a 50/50 hit rate is hardly satisfactory.

The broader implications are highly significant. Mergers and acquisitions are part of the fabric of economic life. They help drive a sizeable proportion of corporate growth, whether in large, mature companies or recent start-ups. Globally, somewhere between 25,000 and 35,000 M&A deals are completed annually. They are not a rare phenomenon.

According to a 2012 study by Sanford C. Bernstein, an equity research firm, the chance of a *Fortune* 1000 company being involved in a merger or acquisition in any given year is close to 30%. Of all the companies that have been listed on the UK stock exchange since 1995, our own research indicated that 25% announced an acquisition within 12 months of listing; by the second year the number rises to 41% and by the third year more than 50%. M&A deals are here to stay.

M&A is one of the most fascinating activities in the business world. However, corporations more often than not get it wrong. We have purposely avoided a bias towards coverage of only private or only public deals – although Chapter 5 on negotiations and Chapter 7 on regulation are more skewed towards the latter – as the mistakes that are often made are the same for both types of deal.

For reasons of data availability and familiarity, the case studies in this book are often of larger deals involving well-known companies. But the lessons learnt from these transactions are applicable to smaller deals between mid-sized or small businesses. Deals between smaller, private companies are often less process-driven and are likely to have fewer issues with regulators and large, diverse shareholder bases than large firms have. Yet in private deals you will probably be negotiating with the business's founders, who may be more emotionally attached to the businesses they have built than the managers of large corporations are. Navigating the politics and dynamics between the parties (when they are very much on opposite sides) at the same time as devising a combined business plan and organisation structure (when these parties have to start working together) is crucial in making sure the deal gets over the line. Dealmakers often say: "A small deal is as complicated and painful as a large one." Simple deals just do not exist.

The M&A process can also be scary, even for experienced dealmakers. As Sebastian James, head of technology retailer Dixons Carphone, said to *Management Today* in 2014 after the merger of Carphone Warehouse and Dixons:

> *My terror was that when we combined the two, we'd get that 80s nightmare where they bred African killer bees with European docile honeybees. You hoped for loads of honey with a nice temperament but you could have wound up with a load of angry bees and not much [of the runny stuff] to show for it.*

The Economist wrote about the challenges of M&A deals in a cover article in September 1994. The article has remained so relevant that they republished it online in November 2014, noting that:

> *It is not so much that marriages result in asset-stripping, as the enemies of takeovers often allege. In aggregate, mergers seldom lead to egregious cuts in R&D, investment or even jobs... Nor is it common for mergers to vindicate the fears of trustbusters, by creating price-rigging monopolies. No, the real disappointment about mergers is that, on average, they do not result in higher profits or greater efficiency; indeed, they often damage these things. And although they prompt a rise in the combined stockmarket value of the merging firms, this gain is often short-lived.*

Although almost all the examples in this book are corporate case studies, there are also obvious lessons that can be learnt for those doing deals in the public sector, such as the merging of governmental agencies, or in the non-profit sector, including the consolidation trend for many charities and hospital trusts. There is a short case study of a charity merger in Chapter 8.

There are lessons to be learnt that will be useful for both seasoned dealmakers and newer participants. The statistics speak for themselves: there is no guarantee you will get your current deal right even if you succeeded with earlier ones. For new dealmakers, this book will take you through the full deal process, from strategic groundwork and doing the right deal, to how to avoid a corporate divorce and what to do if one is inevitable. (Chapter 9 is dedicated solely to the topic of divestitures.) For more experienced dealmakers, a reminder of the dos and don'ts should always come in handy.

Finally, as the authors are located in Europe, there is a natural bias towards case studies where at least one party is European, but there are also examples of deals from North America and elsewhere. We each have first-hand experience in dealmaking worldwide and can testify that the mistakes made are applicable on a global scale. It is probably one of the few areas where culture does not differentiate behaviour.

PART 1

Pre-deal

1

Think before you buy

GETTING TO THE TOP of the corporate ladder puts a bullseye on your back – not just for as long as you are in that job but also afterwards, as CEOs and other senior managers of some failed M&A deals have found to their cost, both reputational and financial. In many jurisdictions, shareholders can file lawsuits against companies and individuals many years after the deals have closed.

As shown in the Introduction, CEOs who make the wrong strategic gamble, as HP's Léo Apotheker did, are summarily fired. There is rightly significant pressure on corporate leaders, commensurate with their often huge remuneration packages, to be seen to deliver quick solutions for their companies. But rushed deals can lead to reputations being destroyed forever – as in the case of RBS's former chief executive, Fred Goodwin (see Chapter 2).

The key phrase above is "to be seen to". This chapter discusses the strategic options open to new CEOs when they take office. But some of these options grab far more attention than others. CEOs are not normally selected as the cover story of magazines like *Forbes* or *Fortune* for achieving years of steady incremental organic growth. But many have appeared on the cover after initiating a transformational merger.

In addition to the high expectations of shareholders, employees, lenders and the press, CEOs who like to do dynamic things are self-selecting. And few corporate decisions are as dynamic as an M&A deal.

In the case of HP, Apotheker was hired not because he was content to do small things, but because he had already been the CEO of SAP, where he had risen up the food chain, in part because of his big, differentiated vision for the company and indeed its role in defining the entire IT sector.

Properly directed, such dynamism can unlock great value for companies and their shareholders through M&A. Unchecked, such dynamic ambition can tip over into the sort of hubris that drove Goodwin towards the decisions that practically destroyed his company when he bought ABN AMRO.

What's your Facebook relationship status?

One of the most successful companies of the past decade and one that has shown it knows when to do M&A – and when not to – is Facebook, the social-media network co-founded by Mark Zuckerberg and four fellow Harvard students. Started in his college dormitory, the company grew phenomenally, with revenues of $12.5 billion at its ten-year anniversary in 2014. Nicely, Facebook's online guide to social status translates into this book's guide to corporate dealmaking.

Facebook allow users to select their relationship status for all their friends to see. The options are:

- Single
- It's complicated
- Open relationship
- Divorced
- Separated
- Widowed
- In a relationship
- Engaged
- Married
- In a domestic partnership
- Civil union

To adapt these options to the corporate world, the options need to be trimmed to five, all of which have a business corollary that any company can consider in its strategic review:

- Single – do nothing, remain independent and focus on organic growth.

- It's complicated – buying minority stakes in other companies or preparing for one of the other four options.

- Open relationship – strategic alliances or joint ventures.

- Divorced – demergers, divestments of assets, liquidation of an unprofitable division or one that is no longer strategically necessary, or in the process of trying to sell a division (separated).

- In a relationship – the start of the process that leads to a formal announcement of an acquisition or merger (engaged), or having done so (married, in a domestic partnership, civil union).

Each of these strategic options is discussed below, but first it is important to stress how little time incoming CEOs may have to make an impact. Bob Kelly, former CEO and chairman of Bank of New York Mellon, was abruptly pushed out by his board following a near-five-year tenure during which he implemented, and then pretty much seamlessly integrated, a widely applauded transformational merger between Bank of New York and Mellon Financial.

The 2011 press release announcing his departure did not provide much detail about his removal, stating simply that it was "due to differences in approach to managing the company" between Kelly and the board of directors. Inevitably there were underlying causes: some observed that there were cultural differences between Kelly and some of his executives and there was also the release of information related to Kelly's decision to pursue publicly a bigger job at Bank of America. But leaving aside any "blame", there is one thing Kelly had in common with many departing executives: he had been in the post for around five years when he left.

The average tenure of a *Fortune* 100 CEO is approximately 4.6 years. Indeed, Kelly used this statistic to answer a question posed to him at a 2010 Cass Business School talk about why he chose to make the huge decision to merge with Bank of New York in 2007 after just nine months in post as CEO and chairman of Mellon Financial. The reality is that public-company boards and institutional shareholders do not have the same generation-long horizons as, say, some investors such as Warren Buffett – and they are even shorter than the five-year standard private equity investment timeframe.

For founder or privately owned high-growth businesses, there usually comes a time when the size of the underlying business means year-on-year growth slows and M&A becomes an important tool to stay ahead of the competition. It is often a strategy used before the company itself is sold and thus demonstrates as well that management can execute deals, which is an attractive feature for later potential buyers, especially for a private equity buyer that wants to continue a "buy-and-build" strategy.

CEOs must decide on their strategy as quickly as possible to have the best hope of reaping the benefits of transaction integration within their corporate lifetime. But M&A is not the only option; there are a number of others, often less risky but equally effective, available to CEOs, as discussed below.

TABLE 1.1 **Corporate status overview**

Status	Company growth	Market position	Market dynamics	Action
Single	Strong	Niche, protected	Medium to strong	Focus on organic growth
It's complicated	Low to strong	Focused	Low to medium	Buying minority stakes in other companies
Open relationship	Low to strong	Focused	Medium to strong	Strategic alliances/joint ventures
Divorced	Low to medium	Diversified	Low to medium	Demerge/divest assets/ liquidate unprofitable division
In a relationship	Low to strong	Expanding	Medium to strong	Focus on M&A

Source: Authors

Staying single

The first option a CEO should consider is to do nothing, at least not a big, external M&A deal, and instead focus on organic growth. In wider society, a "single" Facebook status can carry the taint of social pariah, particularly, perhaps, for the social network's fickle teenage audience.

In the corporate world, however, there are three types of singleton:

- The desperate one who is either a seller but finding it hard to attract a suitor or a buyer who simply can't find a target at an affordable price

- The "catch" at the top of the business hierarchy who can afford to take his or her time to pick and choose between many admirers and targets.

- The fundamentally single, committed corporate bachelors, like many of the new "unicorn" (valuation over $1 billion) private companies in the financial-technology sector and the smaller, often family-owned businesses that prefer the independence of being single.

Over a company's lifetime, it might fall into more than one of these categories at different times.

For a company that came into being only in 2004, Facebook has spent most of its life in the corporate marriage business. Over its relatively short lifetime it has, surprisingly, made more than 50 minor add-on acquisitions as well as some major ones. These were designed to keep things fresh for its crucial teenage audience, and included deals with new social-media platforms Instagram and WhatsApp. But as for being a target, Facebook has been adamant in retaining its single status, even when surrounded by large admirers.

After News Corp bought the MySpace social-networking site in 2005, Facebook became the Prom Queen of a tech sector mesmerised by the corporate marriage business. The company was caught up in a bidding war with several major players, including News Corp, approaching it about a takeover. In 2006, Facebook began formal talks with Yahoo!, whose own strategy was in disarray and who was a deeply eager groom. Yahoo! offered $1.4 billion for Facebook, a fortune for its founder Mark Zuckerberg, who had co-created the social-networking platform as part of a "Would You Rather?" college jape just a few years previously.

So exponential has Facebook's growth been since then, it is easy to forget that at that time the reach of its platform was limited to just university campuses and then high schools in English-speaking countries, principally the US.

Even so, Zuckerberg was not to be diverted from his vision by Yahoo!. Talks broke down and within a year Facebook would receive a $240 million cash injection from Microsoft that allowed Zuckerberg to keep control of the business (and made the Microsoft/Facebook relationship status "it's complicated"). Zuckerberg hit pay dirt in 2012 when the company's flotation catapulted his personal net worth to $28 billion, thanks to his determination to stay corporately single at a crucial time.

In holding out for his vision, Zuckerberg was following in the footsteps of another tech-sector great, Steve Jobs, according to Business Insider, an American business and technology news website.

In the late 1990s Apple was on the verge of bankruptcy. The company had been losing money for 12 years, so it was no great surprise that in 1997 the chief executive, Gil Amelio, was shown the door as the company welcomed back its co-founder, Steve Jobs, who commenced a turnaround that arguably could be the greatest corporate comeback of all time.

The company Jobs had co-created had lost focus and was spending money it did not have on projects that were unlikely to bear fruit. Once a competitor to Microsoft and IBM, Apple had lost the personal computer war. But while Apple still viewed Microsoft and IBM as the enemy, Jobs saw things differently. Instead of selling the company for what would probably have been the equivalent of a corporate pittance, he helped to engineer an emergency $150 million cash injection from Microsoft, which ironically did not want to lose Apple because it believed the US government would come down harder on its own dominant position in software if it were to lose yet another competitor.

Once that lifeline was secured, Jobs began a root-and-branch reform of Apple. At an early meeting he reportedly told the board: "You know what's wrong with this company? The products SUCK. There's no sex in them!" Soon the iMac, the first "non-beige box" computer, was born. Apple sold nearly 800,000 units within five months of launch and by 1998 the company was back in the black. A marketing revolution followed as the iPod, iTunes and finally the iPhone, products with which the old enemy Microsoft had no hope of competing, changed the personal computing market forever.

These examples show that timing is everything when it comes to making a decision about whether to stay single.

When considering whether to merge or buy, sectoral trends can be crucial, whether rivals are consolidating rapidly or whether they are breaking down and demerging. But there may also be overriding company-specific issues, as there were with Facebook. In that case, Zuckerberg was one of the few people in the world who could see his company had a prime-mover advantage in a truly new industry, so he rightly held out as a singleton.

Just because everyone is involved in M&A does not mean that your company should be. Single status may not be bad, as shown above, and it is certainly preferable to being married to the wrong partner.

RBS's 2007 bid for ABN AMRO, a Dutch bank, made sense in terms of rapid sector consolidation and as a defensive move against a rival bid by RBS's competitor, Barclays. But it did not make sense for RBS, which was already overleveraged, to chase ABN AMRO just as the global economy began to unwind, particularly after ABN AMRO completed the lock-up sale of its US arm, LaSalle Bank, supposedly the big prize coveted by the UK bank.

Equally, the converse might be true. The previous wave of UK banking-sector consolidation in the 1990s saw the creation of the successful Lloyds TSB from the merger of the two high-street banks. The spate of deals also provided Fred Goodwin, RBS's CEO at the time, with his greatest triumph in the swift acquisition and integration of a rival, NatWest. That corporate marriage made sense; the next one did not.

Outside these consolidation trends, there is a small band of businesses for which it is always appropriate to stay away from the large, transformational deals. There are not many of them and it is hard to define these committed singletons, since they are not limited to any particular industry or part of the world. Indeed, the essence of their corporate personality is the ability to stay independent in a rapidly globalising world.

A few examples can be found in industries that have already consolidated so deeply that governments and regulators will protect the status quo to ensure they do not become any more concentrated. An example of this is accountancy where, after the collapse of Arthur Andersen made the Big Five a Big Four, regulators have made clear they would save any of the remaining four in the public interest should they suffer a major scandal and that mergers among them will be blocked. Nevertheless, all four accountancy firms have been active in making smaller, bolt-on or complementary/adjacent acquisitions (for example, PricewaterhouseCoopers buying consultant Booz & Co or Deloitte buying Monitor). There are other examples in heavily regulated industries such as mobile and landline telephones and electricity and gas supply. As noted earlier, family-owned business often fall into this category too.

But most committed bachelors are able to stay independent because they have a strategy of providing niche premium products with a global reach. Examples are strategy consultancies, such as McKinsey, Bain and Boston Consulting Group, and certain corporate law firms (see below). Often they provide premium services, particularly in professional services, an overrepresented business among this group.

In the future, increased globalisation, new technology, political revolutions or just the passage of time might force these businesses to adapt. But for now they are single because they can be. And they glory in it.

One such is a New York-based law firm, Wachtell, Lipton, Rosen & Katz. For a business that advises on M&A it represents an anomaly: as resolute a bachelor as exists. So are its leaders ignoring the industry they serve, or is something else going on?

By any measure Wachtell is successful as a stand-alone firm. Founded on a handshake by the four principals and Jerry Kern in 1965, its name has been associated with M&A deals for decades. Wachtell invented the much-copied poison pill, a hostile defence technique that is discussed in Chapter 5.

Wachtell's strategy appears to work, as it has been one of the most profitable corporate law firms in the US since lawyers started keeping public records on performance, with profits per partner of $5 million in 2014, according to *The American Lawyer*. In the same year the firm was the third-most active M&A adviser globally, working on 70 deals worth $308 billion, including Halliburton's acquisition of Baker Hughes for $36.4 billion and the merger of Tim Hortons and Burger King Worldwide, a deal worth $11.4 billion. It is easy to see why Wachtell would neither want nor need to merge with anyone.

Other exceptional law firms have also managed to occupy the same high ground.

In London, Slaughter and May is known as the firm that refused to globalise, or to accept branding developments at a time when its rivals rushed towards globalisation, stealing ideas from other, less traditional, professional service industries along the way. For any other law firm, this refusal to move with the times would have sounded its death knell or it would simply have been absorbed into a larger consolidator.

The secret of Slaughter and May's success is that it advises more of the UK's FTSE 100 and 250 companies than any of its rivals, giving it an in-built advantage over the competition.

As other firms rushed to find international partners, lawyers at Slaughter and May saw the cultures of their rivals being diluted and decided that, as long they did not have to, they did not need to merge. As result of this vote for independence – or, indeed, in spite of it – Slaughter and May has consistently been the most profitable among major European law firms. It has managed to keep its top-notch client base and, perhaps most importantly for those who control the business, its culture.

There are many other professional-services firms and family-owned businesses – small, medium and large – that have remained independent and have been highly successful, mainly because they hold a strong niche position in their industry or within their own geography. Timpson, a UK-wide shoe-repair and key-cutting company, is an excellent example of such a family-owned business (see Chapter 2).

Committed singletons may be admirable high achievers, but singledom is not a reasonable ambition for most companies. The forces of globalisation have been driving businesses towards a "bigger is better" model for decades and will continue to do so.

Thus the more likely scenario is that CEOs will at some point look externally to find growth, innovation or industry-consolidation synergies. However, there are three other Facebook status options that could result in the same outcome and should always be considered first, as they are arguably less risky than full marriage.

It's complicated

In the corporate world, "it's complicated" is analogous to the taking of minority stakes in other companies. As in personal social relationships, this sort of arrangement is increasingly widespread but slightly murky, in that the longer-term purpose of stake-building is often not readily apparent.

In some industries, such as biotechnology and software development, taking minority stakes is an established corporate practice; in others, such as the convergence of banking and technology, it is an emerging, but popular and maybe even necessary, trend. In this sense the corporate world has entered the sphere of venture capitalists en masse, creating seed funds to bankroll start-ups and stakes in emerging players. As with strategic investments in technology start-ups, this is often a form of outsourced R&D for the larger firms.

In the life sciences industry, GlaxoSmithKline spun out a group of scientists and patents involved in experimental drugs for analgesics in 2010. GSK kept 18% of the new business, called Convergence Pharmaceuticals. In this case the deal was seemingly designed to cut overheads in research and development for GSK, boost productivity at the new company and still leave GSK with "skin in the game".

The spin-off was part of wider trend. Big Pharma is facing patent expiry on valuable products and many in the industry have responded to investors' concerns by outsourcing clinical services and research to smaller, more agile, entrepreneurial firms. Baxter spun out Baxalta, its haemophilia treatment division, in 2014; so successful was the spin-off that Baxalta became the target of a successful $32 billion takeover by Shire just 12 months later.

Also in 2014, Euromoney, a business publisher, teamed up with Carlyle, a private equity firm, to buy out data provider Dealogic for $700 million; Euromoney took a 15.5% stake. Here the motivation is less clear. There are some synergies between Dealogic and Euromoney and the publisher could, in the longer term, be planning to buy out Dealogic and move it completely into its stable of titles. Conversely, it could be a purely financial investment. Because it's complicated, nobody really knows.

In other instances, the taking of minority stakes has been followed by a full-blown takeover. This can be a useful tactic for buyers, because minority holdings give their owners important rights and, potentially, crucial influence over and insights into a company. The downside for sellers is that potential buyers can use this strategy to put together a lot of information about your company.

When a bidder knows your company really well, they also know its weaknesses, something that could be helpful at the due diligence phase and ultimately help them in the negotiation phase (see Chapters 3–5). A buyer in the know has a strategic advantage over other bidders, is able to determine better and more quickly the correct value, and is aware of the various issued to be ironed out in the due diligence process.

As discussed in subsequent chapters, momentum is crucial in getting a deal across the line, and an informed buyer has a better understanding of the buttons that need to be pressed to get there. Being able to track the asset for a long time as a minority investor can prove invaluable when a larger transaction process kicks off; it can also deter other potential bidders, as they will be unwilling to invest time in a process that they know they are unlikely to win.

The Glazer family's takeover of Manchester United Football Club in 2005 is a great example of such tactical investment. The family ultimately, and controversially, loaded a previously debt-free business with more than £500 million ($900 million) of debt, some of it in the form of high-interest loan notes issued by hedge funds. In the context of boom-time leveraged buy-outs, the financing structure used by the Glazers to acquire the company with its own money was aggressive, but not unusually so. However, because the takeover was of a football club, and was completed in the teeth of opposition from the fans, it has generated more column inches about debt than many other deals in the decade since it was completed.

In the midst of this furore, one of the more technically interesting aspects of the deal, specifically Malcolm Glazer's acquisition of an ever-increasing minority stake in the club, is often overlooked.

He began to build his stake in Manchester United in March 2003. A year later, despite the steady increase in his holding, Glazer announced that he had "no current intention of making a bid and may reduce his stake". This statement was forced by the UK's Takeover Panel in response to articles in the *Financial Times* and elsewhere stating that he had hired Commerzbank to advise on the possible structure of a takeover.

It is unclear in the context of this statement why Glazer would gradually continue to increase his stake until, in October 2004, his holding approached but did not reach the 30% level at which UK law mandates a full takeover offer.

The Glazer family discussed a bid for the club with its CEO in October 2004. They subsequently relied on the rights and leverage their stake gave them to exert influence over the company, including the removal of three board directors in November of that year (replacing them with their own family members), as they fought a year-long battle to secure full control of the business. Note the information advantage gained by having the three board seats in terms of determining whether to proceed with a highly leveraged offer.

That Glazer initially said he had no plans for a takeover did not stop widespread speculation that this was his intention all along, and that the acquisition of an increasing minority stake was always a tactic to help win the club. In certain circumstances, this would mean that Glazer would have been close to breaching UK laws on takeovers, which probably explains his extensive use of expert advisers.

The Manchester United case is discussed further in Chapter 5.

Open relationship

In the world of personal relationships, an open relationship seems to offer a dazzling chance to have your cake and eat it. In reality, though, such arrangements can turn sour pretty quickly. The corporate version of open relationships – strategic alliances or, more formally, joint ventures (JVs) – can also be challenging. But, done right, they give companies access to industries or markets otherwise out of reach because they lack the necessary local or industry expertise, or the appropriate funding and scale.

The essence of all alliances is the same: two or more corporations agree to operate jointly for a common purpose that they each feel they are unable to achieve alone. There are many casual types of alliance, which are hard to research accurately; this section concentrates on the most formal, measurable type – a JV – where two or more partners invest together in a new vehicle.

There are three main reasons for investing in a JV:

- It allows partners to pool resources. This is particularly useful from a financial perspective when credit is scarce, as in the period immediately following the economic crisis of 2007–08. But it need not be driven by finance; for example, another common driver of a

FIGURE 1.1 **Joint venture rationale**

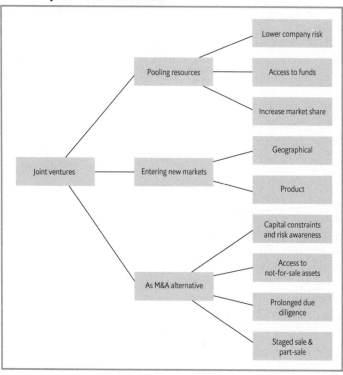

Source: *Sharing Risk: A Study of Corporate Alliances,* Cass Business School, 2009

JV is when companies need access to technologies and skills that cannot be bought. Because of these advantages, even companies that are competitors can team up (as seen earlier with Microsoft and Apple), although careful consideration is needed, as it is difficult to set boundaries regarding what information you share with your partner.

■ It gives partners access to new markets, either geographically or through new products.

■ It is sometimes used as a precursor to M&A, allowing cultural and other due diligence over an extended period.

Unfortunately, as with human open relationships, the corporate version may sound great, but such relationships can be fraught with difficulties and many companies regret entering into them.

How to make JVs work

Comprehensive research by Cass Business School and Allen & Overy, a law firm, of 500 global joint ventures – both large and small – between 1995 and 2014 demonstrates the potential pitfalls of such arrangements. The study found that:

- JVs are not forever – in 60% of cases one or more of the original partners had exited the JV or the JV had been dissolved;
- half of the exited JVs were successful – some 50% ended for a positive reason, but still 46% finished for a negative one such as a dispute (9%) or poor performance (14%);
- JVs are generally a medium-term strategy – a majority (51%) of the exited JVs came to an end within five years of their start date; one year later, 61% were over; 11% had reached their natural or planned end at the time, but in 53% of cases one partner ultimately took control, and in 17% the entire JV was sold to an external party.

Following the study, Allen & Overy made the following recommendations for setting up a JV for success:

- Test your business proposition thoroughly.
- Ensure the strategies of the partners are aligned from the outset; the success of the venture will depend largely on the "fit" of the partners.
- Devise workable decision-making processes.
- In advance, develop a workable exit strategy and dispute resolution procedures.

One company that fell foul of the open relationship is Danone, a French food group, which has made a number of unfortunate JV investments in China, a country where it is notoriously difficult to exit such arrangements.

Danone announced in September 2009 that it was exiting its partnership with Wahaha, a Chinese beverage company. Two years previously the French company had filed lawsuits accusing Wahaha and its founder, Zong Qinghou, of running a parallel copycat production line. Further, Danone alleged that Zong, one of China's richest entrepreneurs, had defrauded it with the help of relatives and a fabricated facade of offshore companies.

To put this in context, Danone and Wahaha had been co-operating since 1996 and their JV was used as a case study for success by business schools.

Serious cracks emerged when Danone tried to buy out Wahaha in 2006 and, according to the *New York Times*, the Chinese company appeared to be holding out for more money. The two sides suspended legal hostilities in late 2007. In 2009, following extensive negotiations, Wahaha bought Danone's 51% stake in the JV. According to analyst estimates, Danone received around $500 million for a business valued at $2 billion.

Another example of the difficulty of exiting an international JV comes from the oil and gas industry. In 2003, BP put its Russian assets into TNK-BP, a JV with the energy oligarchs behind Alfa Group, Access Industries and Renova (AAR). By 2008 AAR was flexing its muscles in a bid to gain greater control of the company; TNK-BP's chief executive, Robert Dudley, fled Russia following what he claimed were politically motivated criminal charges linked to a government-backed campaign of harassment in support of AAR.

In January 2009, BP ceded control over the JV to AAR, whose board had previously been shared 50/50. Two years later the AAR board flexed its muscles again to prevent BP and Russia's former state energy company, Rosneft, from signing a plan to jointly explore for oil and gas in the Russian Arctic.

Only in 2012 was BP able to extract itself from the impasse. AAR agreed to a plan to sell TNK-BP to Rosneft for $55 billion. The deal, which was personally cleared by the Russian president, Vladimir Putin, gave BP $16.7 billion cash and an additional 12.5% stake in Rosneft.

Divorced

Divestment of underperforming assets, demergers and the liquidation of unprofitable divisions are largely outside the scope of this chapter, except insofar as they raise funds that enable refocused companies to go on the acquisition trail, or provide targets for buyers. These issues are discussed in Chapter 9, which covers corporate divorce.

A good example of a demerger is UK confectionery multinational Cadbury's decision to separate out its US drinks business Schweppes in 2008. The sale was designed to raise cash for an acquisition spree, but instead turned Cadbury from predator to prey and ultimately led to its acquisition by Kraft. Sir Dominic Cadbury – although no longer formally part of the company when it was bought – in a talk at Cass Business School following that takeover said that the demerger of Schweppes led to the ability of a larger food company to do a "pure-play acquisition" to buy the confectioner founded by his great-grandfather.

In May 2003, Todd Stitzer took over as CEO at Cadbury Schweppes, then a drifting food and drinks company comprising two ill-fitting halves: a global confectionery business and a US and European drinks business whose main brands were Dr Pepper, Snapple and Oasis. Although the acquisition of Adams in 2002 had made Cadbury Schweppes the world's biggest confectionery group, its global market share of the wider sector was only 10%, hardly a commanding position.

The company had long dreamed of dominating the confectionery business through a merger with Hershey and in 2002 had tried but failed, when the US company's controlling charitable trust stopped the deal at the last minute. Cadbury Schweppes lacked the funds for a proper spending spree, so it sold its European drinks brands, Orangina and Oasis, to Lion Capital in a first step to raise cash.

Nelson Peltz, a US activist investor, began taking an interest in the sector, buying stakes in Cadbury and, unbeknown to the UK company, in its rival, Kraft. Peltz's plans for Cadbury, to use it in industry consolidation, seemed to chime with those of Stitzer and the Cadbury board, so the UK company began slowly to discuss how to sell off its US drinks businesses, while privately reopening talks with Hershey in the hope of getting the trust onside with a proposed merger of equals. But Cadbury's US shareholders were pushing for an immediate split.

Having failed to find a private equity buyer for the drinks business, the board was pushed into a US listing far sooner than it would have liked. In 2008, the Dr Pepper Snapple Group was listed in the US, bringing in cash that left Cadbury especially vulnerable to a takeover bid. Today the "unwanted" drinks arm remains an independent business, while the "jewel in the crown", the Cadbury confectionery arm, was bought by Peltz's other target, Kraft, in 2009.

In a relationship

Once all other relationship options have been carefully considered, it is time for ambitious companies that still see a merger or takeover as the best option to get engaged – that is, make an offer – and progress to marriage. This is the subject of most of the rest of this book: what can go wrong in a corporate marriage, but also what can be done to avoid the main pitfalls and ultimately make it work. This can include the time when the companies are just talking to each other, seriously considering joining together (in a relationship), formally agreeing to merge (engaged), or finally getting married.

First-mover advantage

A 2009 study on European CEO succession and M&A strategy by the M&A Research Centre at Cass Business School suggests that an early, focused acquisition is the optimal action for many companies.

Analysing CEOs in four European countries (the UK, France, Germany and Spain), the study found that those CEOs who were hired with a clear mandate for change were, unsurprisingly, the most likely to act quickly, within a year, to do their first M&A deal.

Those who embarked on dealmaking in that first year bought assets more frequently than they sold them. An analysis of company share price found that CEOs hired by poorly performing companies (defined by weaker share-price performance compared with their peers) tended to be those who sold rather than bought assets.

Although CEOs who sold assets benefited from a short-term bump as cash flooded into the company, often this was simply a quick fix that did not assist growth over the medium or longer term. In the longer run, the most successful strategy is buying in the first year.

However, while the optimal strategy is to buy early, CEOs should be careful not to overextend themselves. The study also found that CEOs who bought more than one company in their maiden 12 months saw a decrease in corporate returns over the long run.

As shown throughout this book, CEOs with a clear strategy who act quickly and decisively to merge, and implement their decision using best practice, are well placed to add value for their companies. After all, ambitious businesses, just as much as teenagers, often want and need to be in a relationship.

Think before you buy: dos and don'ts

- **Do** first consider the alternatives to M&A – several options are available and they can be less risky than a takeover.

- **Don't** enter into a JV or alliance before being comfortable – in principle and legally – that your and your partner's intentions are aligned.

- **Do** consider divestments as a strategic option, as it can be more efficient to divest a division that is non-core than to buy additional capabilities to make it grow.

- **Do** be prepared for M&A – it is rare to stay single throughout your corporate life.

2

Avoid tunnel vision

YOU HAVE RUN THROUGH THE OPTIONS and you believe that M&A is an answer to your company's strategic needs. At this point, you have to get the two fundamental foundations of successful M&A right. This means first formulating the best possible deal strategy and then putting in place an optimal target-selection procedure. The former is a precursor to long-term success; the latter determines whether companies can implement that strategy day in, day out, long before they move on to the detail of due diligence (see Chapter 3). Of the three big mistakes of dealmaking, this chapter is about planning.

At this stage you are trying to lay the foundations for your company's success in M&A, and good planning is crucial. As Paul Walsh, former chief executive of Diageo, a UK-based global beverages company, advises:

> Unless you have a coherent business strategy, it's very hard to have a coherent M&A strategy. If that strategic intent is bought into by the board and employees, the M&A stuff follows easily.

Generally, because the worst examples illustrate these points the most dramatically, many case studies in this book are object lessons in how not to approach M&A. But this does not present a fair picture of the real world. M&A is an important driver of corporate and economic growth; it is something that companies frequently do get right. Yet finding a poster child for successful M&A still remains much harder than finding a cautionary tale. And any "success" can only be measured in a medium-term window after the transaction has bedded in and before unforeseeable factors – unrelated and unable to be anticipated at the time of the deal, such as fundamentally new developments in technology or global geopolitics – create a different yardstick.

Looking at the period since 2008, Diageo is one company that did get it right. At the conceptual stage it formulated the right strategy for the company and then it implemented that strategy well, getting the fine detail right. The company achieved every "do" in this chapter's M&A checklist. It was determined, yet flexible, in implementing its M&A policy, chasing down targets for years after first identifying them and then preparing in detail for tough negotiations.

Deal strategy

M&A is in Diageo's DNA. At the heart of the company are its two forebears, Guinness and Grand Metropolitan, two UK-listed food and drinks conglomerates that merged in 1997. Diageo's grandparents, Arthur Bell & Sons (Bell's whisky-maker) and International Distillers & Vintners, are still recognisable in parts of the business.

Think about Diageo today and Johnnie Walker, Smirnoff, Ypióca (if you are Brazilian) or Yeni Raki (if you are Turkish) come to mind – all leading beverage alcohol brands with a global or strong regional reach that Diageo has brought under its roof as part of a coherent M&A strategy.

The conglomerate's former chief executive, Paul Walsh, who led the company from 2000 to 2013, had a key role in designing that strategy supported by a capable senior-management team. One of his first actions was to conduct a strategic review that put his acquisition policy at the heart of the company. From 2000, the company had clearly defined ambitions and was quickly mapping out the M&A paths by which to reach them. During Walsh's tenure Diageo's share price nearly quadrupled, and much of that rise recorded in later years as corporate strategy was executed through dealmaking.

As discussed in Chapter 1, new CEOs often do major deals in their first year because they are brought in with a mandate for change. For Walsh, thinking about M&A came even earlier. Asked to consider the top job a year ahead, he replied that he would happily take it, but believed the company as currently configured was not a global winner.

At this juncture, before embarking on a programme of acquisitions, a board should consider the full range of strategic options from disposals to a joint venture. In an interview for this book, Walsh said:

Diageo had not long been created when I took over. We had four unamalgamated divisions: fast food (the Burger King outlets), Pillsbury convenience food, spirits and Guinness. In my opinion every one of them was sub-scale. I thought we had done a good job on food improving the scale and margins, but there was no way I could see us getting into the Premier League of food players.

The central tenet of the strategic review was fundamentally to reposition Diageo through an acquisition spree. The company saw that for a modern, amalgamated "house of brands", production and distribution were no longer the central purpose; marketing, tapping into the lifestyle aspirations of consumers and cross-distribution were crucial. For that, Diageo needed to focus solely on alcohol, target recognisable luxury brands and, later on, attract the growing middle classes of the southern hemisphere.

Diageo's emerging-markets acquisition strategy would reach its pinnacle between 2008 and 2013, as the company shifted investment geographically south. But it was Walsh's early work that laid the foundations for the later focused acquisitions. In 2000, the company manifestly needed to divest to raise cash and concentrate on its core drinks assets. By the end of the year, it had sold its food division, Pillsbury – which included breakfast cereals such as Cheerios – to rival General Mills for $10.5 billion.

Two years later Diageo sold Burger King to TPG, a US private equity firm, for $1.5 billion. This deal, which took two and half years to complete – during which time both Burger King's performance and the prospects for the fast-food industry had deteriorated – was criticised by some people, who thought the company had accepted a bargain basement price. But, freed from its unwanted food interests, Diageo was now in a position to make the acquisitions necessary in its new core. Walsh noted this when he said, "There are times in life it is better to be quick than good. We were very fortunate."

When Seagram's spirits and wine portfolio was put up for auction by Vivendi Universal in 2001, it represented a rare opportunity to participate in industry consolidation that few of Diageo's rivals were ready for. Diageo, however, was.

Partnering with Pernod gave Diageo the cash to get a deal for the whole of Seagram done quickly. The two companies tabled a winning $8.15 billion bid and shared the spoils, with Diageo taking the Captain Morgan rum brand it coveted. These early deals, on which he staked his career, gave Walsh a strong power base that allowed Diageo later to build its emerging-markets business – an area it felt was underrepresented in its corporate portfolio of brands. Walsh noted:

> Buying Seagram and selling Pillsbury were the "bet the ranch" deals. My position wasn't at stake in the same way during subsequent deals, even though there were some very large ones.

The first step to formulating an optimum strategy is selecting the right chief executive. For Diageo, Walsh was the right person at the right time, as shown above. A Diageo lifer, he began his career at Grand Metropolitan and knew the business and its people intimately. This experience helped him to make good decisions on deal strategy and gave him the strength to persuade the board to opt for his divestiture programme when just a few years earlier the company – and Walsh himself – had been building up its food divisions.

To see what happens when an executive attempts a transformational deal at a time of huge uncertainty, look no further than RBS, whose chief executive, Fred Goodwin, pushed through the acquisition of ABN AMRO, purchased jointly with a financial services company, Fortis (of Belgium and the Netherlands), and Banco Santander (of Spain).

"The world's biggest ever cross-border acquisition", "the banking sector's largest ever deal", "the deal that nearly 'bankrupted' Britain": RBS's acquisition of ABN AMRO was a deal for which no superlative seems enough. "[The ABN AMRO acquisition] is a serious indictment of both the senior management and leadership," according to the UK government's Treasury Select Committee analysis of the Financial Services Authority (FSA) report on the failure of RBS.

The takeover Goodwin drove through was a massive failure in one of the industries most likely to damage the wider public good, at a time when the financial system was creaking. Two of the three co-acquirers – RBS and Fortis – had to be bailed out by their governments in the wake of the hostile deal, so on that measure alone it may be the worst takeover in history.

The FSA, the UK regulator that has since been disbanded in part because of its failure to properly regulate RBS, said this about the takeover:

> *The acquisition of ABN AMRO by a consortium led by RBS greatly increased RBS's vulnerability. The decision to fund the acquisition primarily with debt, the majority of which was short-term, rather than equity eroded RBS's capital adequacy ... In the circumstances of the crisis, its role as the leader of the consortium affected market confidence in RBS.*

Goodwin and two former RBS chairmen, Sir Tom McKillop and Sir George Mathewson, were held jointly responsible for the failure, but it was Goodwin – who was stripped of his knighthood because of the fallout from the failed acquisition – who was Public Enemy Number One in the wake of the deal.

Could it have been foreseen or is it just a case of 20/20 hindsight?

A few industry mavens had been warning about Goodwin's style for years. One example from 2005 was James Eden, an outspoken but highly rated banking analyst at Dresdner Kleinwort Wasserstein, who questioned Sir George at an analyst meeting following RBS's acquisition of Charter One in the US. "Some of our investors think Sir Fred is a megalomaniac who cares more about size than shareholder value," the *Daily Telegraph* reported Eden telling Sir George as investors rebelled over the arguably overpriced Charter One deal.

Ironically, Goodwin's fall from grace was almost certainly built on his initial success. In banking circles he was considered a Scottish upstart in the City. He started out as an accountant at Touche Ross before taking over as deputy chief executive of Clydesdale, a small Scottish bank owned by National Australia Bank (NAB). When Sir George poached him to be deputy chief executive of RBS in 1998, he was already known as "The Shred" thanks to his abrasive cost-cutting style. Goodwin's role in RBS's takeover of NatWest – still considered one of the best deals in the UK banking industry – set him up in an elevated position.

In September 1999, NatWest had been due to merge with Legal & General, an insurance company. But investors hated the deal and forced out the bank's chief executive, Sir Derek Wanless, leaving it rudderless. RBS pursued friendly talks with Bank of Scotland, but Sir George and Goodwin were plotting a rival offer for NatWest.

The FSA backed this view, saying:

RBS's track record of successful acquisitions and integration, particularly of National Westminster Bank (NatWest), may have led the RBS executive management to be confident in its ability to integrate the ABN AMRO business. It is clear that RBS underestimated the operational and integration risks that arose from the acquisition.

One of the prime architects of the ABN AMRO deal, RBS's former global head of investment banking, Johnny Cameron, echoed these sentiments when he later spoke to FSA officials as part of the inquiry:

After we bought NatWest, we had lots of surprises, but almost all of them were pleasant. And I think that lulled us into a sense of complacency around that.

Goodwin went on to deliver not only the takeover, but also £3 billion ($6.2 billion) of post-integration synergies. Once Sir George was elevated from chief executive to chairman – a move that goes against the standards of UK corporate governance norms – his protégé cemented his position further.

There is no question that corporate governance practices at RBS were partly to blame for the failure of the ABN AMRO deal. Having a non-biased accountable board with relevant experience and expertise that can challenge management is crucial in getting a deal right. In particular, it helps executives not to get too emotionally attached to a deal or a particular target and thus avoids tunnel vision.

There are also useful lessons here for small and medium-sized businesses. For smaller, often non-public companies, having board members with experience in dealmaking is equally important, though for slightly different reasons. Senior executives in such businesses are often more operationally involved and therefore have less time to meet with and get to know potential target companies.

Having experienced board members (often the chairman) to navigate the more difficult discussions with counterparties, both target companies and potential investors, can be helpful to keep relationships intact. Thus growing companies often seek board members with such experience, often as non-executives or independent board members or, in the case of family-owned businesses, an advisory board.

Target selection

In the selection of targets, companies put into practice their well-thought-out, coherent deal strategies. This work goes on not just immediately ahead of a deal, but day in, day out, for years. It is in this sphere that Diageo truly excelled.

Diageo built on its early M&A success. The company's transformational deal with Seagram had helped it to position itself, particularly in the US, but by 2009 it had become clear that Diageo was too dependent for revenue on developed markets, particularly in Europe. Around two-thirds of its revenues were from North America and western Europe at a time when growth was stagnating in both regions in the wake of the credit crisis.

At the same time, emerging markets were booming. As Jim O'Neill, chief economist at Goldman Sachs, coined the acronym BRIC (Brazil, Russia, India and China), so Diageo began to focus beyond its established markets for growth, kicking off a strategic project to help it identify the best regions for fresh investment.

It decided to target the emerging middle class in Latin America, Asia, Africa and Russia/eastern Europe. Such consumers were identified as households with an annual income of between $5,000 and $35,000, entering an income bracket where they could afford to think beyond meeting their basic needs and become aspirational in their way of living.

Explaining his thinking at the time, Walsh said:

We had been looking at emerging markets before then, but in 2008–09, it was clear the world was going to change. It was my belief and the board supported it that Europe was going to be lacklustre for a period of time.

He added:

The way to offset that was to harness the economic power in these new markets. As I stand here today when we have seen some of the bloom come off that rose, I still believe that one of the few things you should not bet against in economic theory are demographic trends. When you combine those with even modest per capita gap growth, you get a very exciting story.

TABLE 2.1 **Diageo's deal process**

Steps	Description
1 Ideas generation/sourcing	Executive Committee strategy, local market strategies, global category strategies, M&A team reviews and advisers. All with the aim of demonstrating a compelling opportunity.
2 Issuing project alerts	■ Documenting strategic rationale, preliminary financial returns, investment dashboard, early assessment of deal issues and RASCI (parties responsible, accountable, supporting, consulting and informed) ■ Request authority from CEO/CFO to start negotiation process
3 Dealmaking	■ Project valuation ■ Project negotiation ■ Perform due diligence on target ■ Project integration planning
4 Project approvals	■ Final approval request to CEO/CFO and Board of Directors
5 Post-deal completion reviews	The first review is done one year after the deal is completed while a second review is done three to four years post-completion

Source: *Seeking growth: A case study of Diageo Plc's growth strategy in emerging markets*, Cass Business School, 2015

In 2009, Diageo set out to reach a 50/50 split in terms of revenue generated from developed and emerging markets, and since then has focused most of its acquisitions in the latter. The right target companies would provide access to the targeted consumers and would help to build Diageo's distribution network in areas of the world where it was not possible do so as quickly organically, boosting overall corporate integration. Perhaps best of all, there were several potential targets in most markets, all medium-sized bolt-on acquisitions, so it made target selection much easier. If Diageo selected the right acquisitions and remembered not to get fixated on just one, it need not overpay.

Having spent the previous nine years heavily involved in M&A, in 2009 Walsh was well placed for the next round of acquisitions, with the confidence of the board, investors, staff and advisers. The company had also designed its own comprehensive system to run a deal project (see Table 2.1).

Diageo says *saúde* to Ypióca

On May 12th 2012, Diageo issued a press release announcing a deal with Brazil's Ypióca Agroindustrial to acquire its leading drinks brand for £300 million ($438 million). A textbook acquisition from its emerging-markets period, this is a prime example of Diageo's tenacity in M&A and is equally useful as a case study to show how a medium-sized company can "sell" itself or its divisions to a larger company.

In the decade leading up to 2008, the Brazilian economy had been transformed and was now among the ten biggest in the world. With a young population – 50% of Brazilians were under the age of 29 at the time – the country's demographics promised an economic boom that would create exactly the growing aspirational middle class with disposable income that Diageo sought.

It was estimated that 57% of the population – or 113 million Brazilians – would be middle-class by 2014, the year Brazil was to host the World Cup, with more joining their ranks by 2016, when Brazil would host the Olympic Games. Those two sporting events were in themselves expected to increase the country's consumption of beverage alcohol significantly.

Diageo focused on cachaça, a Latin American spirit used in caipirinha cocktails, as the best prospective investment. Cachaça, Brazil's national drink, is a spirit distilled from fermented sugar-cane juice and has dominated the local market for about 500 years. Consumption was almost exclusively domestic, but sales of the premium segment were growing and Diageo believed it could adapt its vast knowledge of other global brands, as well as other national drinks such as Mey İçki raki in Turkey and Zacapa rum in Guatemala.

Brazil has over 4,000 different brands of cachaça and Diageo's preferred choice was the high-quality Ypióca. The target was an attractive brand with the obvious additional appeal of a distribution network in the north-eastern region of Brazil that Diageo could leverage to drive sales not only for Johnnie Walker whisky and Smirnoff vodka, but also for its other emerging middle-class-targeted brands.

When Diageo first approached the owners to explore a deal, the analysis, valuation and due diligence took longer and were more complex than initially expected because the assets had to be carved out of Ypióca Agroindustrial. Diageo therefore continued to keep its options open throughout in case the deal did not proceed.

ABN AMRO: it's hard to see what's in it

There is also a wrong way to do it. In its bid for ABN AMRO, RBS got fixated on a single target, made a takeover decision seemingly based on emotion and hubris, and turned up to a sale late. Not a good combination.

In January 2007, as RBS's investment banking adviser, Merrill Lynch, briefed it on a plan to lead a break-up bid for ABN AMRO, Goodwin's power was unchallenged (see above).

Analysts had long suspected that ABN AMRO was the banking sector's next takeover target. This was confirmed as London-based hedge funds, including Toscafund, then run by the now-retired former RBS chairman, Sir George Mathewson, began to take stakes in the bank. Unfortunately for Goodwin and unbeknown to him, ABN AMRO had already met just days earlier with his UK rival, John Varley, chief executive of Barclays Bank, to discuss a consensual takeover. Being late to a takeover party is often fatal and, in this instance, ABN AMRO's chief executive, Rijkman Groenink, told Goodwin that his bank was not for sale, even as he discussed terms with Varley.

On March 18th Barclays gave Varley approval to pursue a takeover and the story broke in the UK press shortly thereafter.

RBS, knowing that an outright bid for ABN AMRO would be blocked on antitrust grounds, began to assemble a raiding party that ultimately comprised Fortis and Santander. The latter was a long-term investor in RBS, with a seat on its board. Despite the fact that they had had no access to confidential ABN AMRO information – particularly important in financial sector deals but critical for proper due diligence and pricing in any deal – and that Barclays did have such access, as they were well into their due diligence process, the consortium launched a hostile bid on April 15th at a higher price than that of their rivals.

The decision to proceed without due diligence is ultimately what cost RBS its solvency because ABN AMRO's investment banking division contained some of the most toxic subprime debt around. Due diligence is discussed in Chapter 3, but here it is indicative of a more fundamental problem: CEO hubris. RBS's decision surprised the market. The issue of due diligence – or rather the lack of it – was singled out by the FSA retrospectively as one of the biggest problems with the deal:

> *In proceeding on that basis, however, RBS's board does not appear to have been sufficiently sensitive to the wholly exceptional and unique importance of customer and counter-party confidence in a bank. As a result, in the [FSA] Review Team's view, the board's decision-making was defective at the time.*

One important element of the deal for RBS was ABN AMRO's US arm, LaSalle Bank, a better business than RBS's own Citizens Financial Group (itself an RBS acquisition made in 1988). Realising this, ABN AMRO adopted a lock-up sale defence: it sold what the unwanted bidder wanted most. ABN agreed to sell LaSalle to Bank of America, thereby making it impossible for RBS, if it successfully bought ABN AMRO, to merge LaSalle with Citizens.

Yet RBS continued to pursue ABN AMRO, re-justifying its strategy on the strength of synergies between ABN's investment banking operations and RBS's similar global banking and markets business.

As spring turned into summer, RBS may – or may not – have tried to get out of the takeover, but the bid stood. Commentators in the UK press thought RBS and Goodwin were out of control. In July 2007 James Harding, then business editor of *The Times*, said:

> *For RBS, the task is to convince its own shareholders the bid is still worth the candle now that LaSalle is lost... Someone will lose. And if it's hard to see why [Barclay's boss] Varley is staking his reputation on ABN, it's now even harder to see what's in it for Sir Fred – other than winning.*

Barclays, perhaps because of what it had seen inside ABN AMRO, did not increase its opening offer. In September 2007 RBS's bid for ABN AMRO closed, and RBS was finally able to see what it had bought. As the financial crisis continued, it found that it had bought a bank full of dangerous liabilities.

Before the deal closed, the governments of the Netherlands and Belgium had to partly nationalise Fortis, RBS's partner. RBS, which was thinly capitalised and had financed the acquisition through the failing wholesale credit markets, was well on its way to the same fate.

How to recover from deals that are going wrong is discussed in the rest of this book. In this case there was almost certainly only one way to recover: to walk away. By not counter-bidding Barclays did walk away, and it helped the bank avoid compulsory nationalisation when its biggest rival had to be bailed out. Sometimes the best deals are those not done.

Patience is the watchword: Diageo says *şerefe* to Mey İçki

If you really want an asset, your corporate ambition need not put you at a disadvantage. One of Diageo's first emerging-market acquisitions, Mey İçki, a Turkish beverage alcohol company, demonstrates that if you really want something, you must play a long, dispassionate game.

As part of the process of moving further into emerging markets, Diageo had identified Turkey as one of the target countries. It was, in many ways, even more attractive than Brazil, as it already had a fast-growing middle class with consumer spending forecast to grow at 6% a year – twice the rate of GDP – by 2010.

When the Turkish government privatised Mey İçki in 2004 as part of its sale of TEKEL, a tobacco and alcoholic beverages company, Diageo considered it a possible investment opportunity. Mey İçki, which was in need of a more modern management, was eventually sold to TPG, a US private equity group – but Diageo had not forgotten about it.

When it decided to exit the business in 2010, TPG (which had bought Burger King from Walsh eight years previously) remembered Diageo's interest in Mey İçki. By this point TPG had transformed the company, creating a world-class distribution system that Diageo could use for its international brands. However, as Mey İçki was in the preliminary stages of an initial public offering (IPO), TPG wanted the full market price. At the same time, the deal was one of the largest Diageo had executed in an emerging country for many years, and for its strategy to be successful it needed a totally reliable asset. This meant that it was more flexible on price than usual.

Keeping an open mind, Diageo considered the potential scale of the local raki spirit market including the local political and economic conditions, which were crucial for a company buying a manufacturer and distributor of alcohol in a country where the majority of the population was Muslim. Diageo was able to negotiate price with TPG, but knowing the worth of Mey İçki to its emerging-market strategy, it took a balanced approach, making sure that the price was not too far below TPG's expected IPO valuation.

Eventually, a deal was announced in February 2011. The cost to Diageo was $2.1 billion – 9.9 times Mey İçki's 2010 EBITDA – a full price, but at a level where Diageo was still a keen buyer.

Has the bloom gone at Diageo?

For the purposes of M&A strategy, Diageo's success is discussed within a particular timeframe, in this case 2000–13. Although Diageo had nearly reached its target of earning 50% of its global revenues from emerging markets by the end of 2014, profit growth outside Europe and the US had begun to fluctuate. Some of the reasons for this were beyond Diageo's control, such as weakening currencies in South Africa, Turkey and Venezuela and an anti-extravagance crackdown in China that reduced demand in that country for its premium spirits.

This does not negate the company's success. Walsh, who after leaving Diageo became non-executive chairman at Compass, a multinational food group, said in 2015:

> Diageo is in a phase whereby there is not just economic uncertainty,
> but also political and security uncertainty. So we are inevitably
> going to see volatility, but you still can't bet against those long-term
> demographics.

What is clear is that overall emerging-market acquisitions helped to transform Diageo from a North Atlantic company to a global leader. Perhaps most importantly, the company decided what was the best thing to do based on the information it had at the time and implemented that decision with unusual rigour.

In this regard, it is useful to consider the differences between emerging and more developed markets. Allan Taylor, M&A partner at global law firm White & Case, noted:

> *In emerging markets, generally the deals are more likely to fail due to the seller and buyer taking a very different view of the market growth potential of the target. When combined with different risk appetites for due diligence issues, execution certainty and market risks, this can create a real potential for serious disagreement regarding pricing and willingness to commit fully.*

However, he went on to say:

> *In developed markets we tend to see deals failing due to a loss of momentum caused by lack of internal support and lack of certainty about being able to achieve strategic premiums. That comes down to planning and leadership of the key people. In public markets with share-for-share deals, there is also the issue of properly communicating synergies to the market and the ability for target shareholders to see upside in the combined entity; bidders must ensure that they effectively sell the benefits of the acquisition to the target board and shareholders and other key stakeholders.*

As discussed in Chapter 6, such communication is crucial. Lack of communication is one of the big three mistakes that should be avoided.

Small, family-owned businesses can do this well, even when staying local. Timpson traces its origins back to 1865, when William Timpson opened a shoe shop in Manchester. It is still a family-owned company, but it has expanded throughout the UK, through acquisition, into key cutting, watch repairs, engraving, dry cleaning and photo processing. Although these may not seem to be linked, the selection of acquisition targets follows a formula. The preferred targets are businesses in distress.

As John Timpson, great-great grandson of the founder, explains:

> *We try not to buy anything that's doing very well. You've got to pay a lot of money and then you've got to do it better than someone who was*

FIGURE 2.1 **Target selection process: the 100:1 ratio**

100 possible targets	Drawing up the long list of possible targets of interest
25 companies reviewed by external analysis only	Research and due diligence done without contacting the company
10 approached with minimal contact	Target approached indirectly via an adviser to determine availability; limited due diligence done through advisers, if possible, or from public sources
4 targets approached via direct contact	Extensive due diligence performed; limited initial feelers extended regarding price and terms
2 progress to deal discussions	Discussions about price and purchase terms to reach a deal
1 deal, to be accepted and agreed	But there are still risks to the deal, as the target still needs to accept the offer; a last-minute outbidding by a competitor is also possible

Source: Authors

doing quite well before. It's much easier to do a great deal when buying a crap business; we want to be the last man standing in an industry that no one else likes.

For example, in late 2008 Timpson bought 187 of Max Spielmann's photo-processing stores out of administration for £1.3 million ($1.9 million), substantially expanding its own coverage in England and Scotland, and taking on 545 employees. But 127 stores were not purchased, as these did not meet Timpson's rigorous selection criteria. Within eight months, the purchase price had been recovered from the profits generated by the 187 stores.

Frequent buyers who get their deal strategy right will know and appreciate the value of maintaining a "live" list of possible targets. The number of potential targets a company needs to review to reach a completed deal obviously differs from time to time, but as a rough estimate, a 100:1 ratio is a good benchmark (see Figure 2.1).

As seen in the RBS/ABN AMRO case, becoming fixated on a particular target or situation can be dangerous, so maintaining a list of possible alternatives is crucial. A well-defined and mapped target list will also help identify priority companies in which it is worth investing more time to ensure that you are well placed as a bidder when the possibility of a deal arises.

Avoid tunnel vision: dos and don'ts

Setting the M&A strategy

- **Do** have a clearly defined M&A strategy on which the board and the CEO are aligned.
- **Do** be explicit about what each potential target will contribute to your overall corporate strategy and have options.
- **Do** have good corporate governance structures in place including strong and experienced non-executive directors: CEOs who simply hear confirmation of their own ideas will make bad decisions.

Implementing your strategy

- **Do** stay flexible – more than one takeover target can often fulfil the same strategic aim.
- **Don't** get fixated on a single target – this means looking at some 100 targets for every one you buy.
- **Do** be committed to delivering on your M&A strategy.
- **Don't** make a takeover decision based on emotion or hubris.
- **Do** be prepared to chase a target for many years once you have identified it.
- **Don't** be late in a takeover battle – you will rarely win even if you do acquire the target.

3

Knowledge is power

WHEN THE FINANCIAL SERVICES AUTHORITY, then the UK's financial regulator, began the first of many reviews of RBS's catastrophic takeover of ABN AMRO, it described the British bank's due diligence on its target as "minimal". That any buyer – let alone one of the world's biggest banks – could be satisfied to proceed with a takeover after only a minimal assessment of the hugely complex financial instruments held by its target is mind-boggling. It is safe to say that RBS's due diligence on ABN AMRO was a complete failure, as quickly became clear when RBS took control and discovered the bank was riddled with toxic debt.

Numerous buyers have begun on a much stronger footing than RBS – many with a reasonably solid M&A vision – but ultimately their acquisitions have failed to bear financial fruit because of mistakes at the due diligence stage. This is true whether the target is large or small; you should not assume that because an acquisition is small the process is easier.

In the takeover failures discussed in this book, mistakes during the due diligence phase were often either the underlying cause, or at the least the final nail in the coffin. Due diligence may be seen as the dull sibling of other more newsworthy areas of M&A, such as regulatory battles or hostile bid tactics, but things often go wrong for the buyer in the data room.

To avoid the three big mistakes of dealmaking, at this stage all eyes should be on planning and people. Doing the right level of due diligence should be part of a company's broader M&A plan and, if it is done properly, the information gleaned will continue to be useful through the integration phase and beyond. Within this, it is important that due diligence also covers the target company's people and culture;

after all, the "assets" that walk out of the door and go home every night are often a company's most valuable ones. The cultural implications of a corporate marriage are among the most important determinants of deal success, yet they are often overlooked in the due diligence process.

When a bid is hostile – as in the case of RBS's bid for ABN AMRO – a lack of due diligence is a risk that is knowingly taken and should be fully understood as making the takeover more risky and prone to mistakes. But even when the target provides full access, full due diligence should be conducted. Often, friendly "full access" can lull a buyer into believing that it can put off due diligence until late in the process. This can be particularly true with deals between two smaller companies that know each other well from the market and are making a friendly deal to merge. But even in larger deals when an approach is friendly – so proper time and access to due diligence is available – there is little excuse for these types of errors. Yet they still happen, as in the Volkswagen/Rolls-Royce deal discussed below.

Sometimes particular circumstances dictate that a transaction must be hurried (see the Britvic case study later in this chapter), but here the expectation is that the buyer has enough pre-existing research or industry expertise in its locker to be able to pull the deal off. And it should do so with eyes wide open.

This chapter provides an overview of the pre-announcement due diligence process, and touches on what is different in cross-border M&A. In terms of the three big mistakes of dealmaking, bad due diligence often centres on two potential problems in particular: poor planning and poor people management.

Due diligence is totally intertwined with fixing the correct value of the target, a function that can properly be finalised only at the end of the due diligence process. A thorough approach will give a bidder the appropriate foundation in fixing the correct price. For this reason, this chapter and the next one on valuation should be read together.

Where is diligence most due?

Performing thorough due diligence is critical to ensure deal success. It tends to focus on the buyer reviewing documentation and interviewing stakeholders about the target, but a good due diligence process also involves the target firm assessing the style and intention of the bidder.

FIGURE 3.1 **Areas of due diligence**

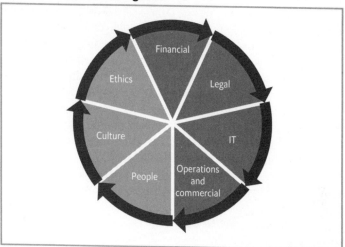

Source: Authors

Traditionally, due diligence has been confined to tangible disciplines, primarily financial, legal, IT, operations and commercial. Conducting a takeover only through that narrow prism, however, can be damaging; "softer" issues such as people and governance, culture and ethics are equally important (see lighter shaded categories in Figure 3.1). Poor due diligence and a lack of understanding of the correct valuation of soft assets such as management and employee retention created huge losses for shareholders in cases such as Hewlett-Packard's takeover of Autonomy (discussed in the Introduction) or Microsoft's acquisition of Nokia.

New systems for measuring intellectual property (IP) and intangibles have been created to deal with such failures as the corporate world has moved on. Other risk factors, such as cyber-security, have already found a place on the due diligence checklist, following a number of high-profile cases, such as adultery website Ashley Madison's planned IPO in 2015 before it was very publicly hacked. This area of cyber-security has also been critical in M&A deals ranging from the retail industry to financial services, in both public and private deals.

Another example of emerging due diligence is a company's social-media policies and footprint. A target's social-media presence on Twitter, Facebook and other platforms should come under as much scrutiny as other areas of due diligence. This is especially important as often these new-media areas are run by younger, less experienced staff in teams that may work online remotely, not within the corporate headquarters, and thus would not normally be included in the due diligence process. For many companies, their online presence is their shop front for many, if not most, of their customers.

Yet it is important to remember that there are still many pitfalls, even in "traditional" due diligence.

If you buy a Rolls-Royce car today, it will have been manufactured in Goodwood, UK. But you will be buying it from BMW, a German automobile company, which took control of Rolls-Royce in 2003. Had M&A history gone to plan, you would be buying the car from BMW's bitter rival, Volkswagen. The failed Rolls-Royce/Volkswagen deal represents what many would call one of the worst IP mistakes in history.

In 1998, Vickers, a UK manufacturing company that had owned the Rolls-Royce and Bentley brands since 1906, was struggling to keep its business going. Other UK car manufacturers had sold their businesses to European and US rivals decades earlier, and there was much national gnashing of teeth as Vickers moved to sell off one of the final bits of the UK's proud automotive history.

Production of expensive Rolls-Royces and Bentleys had fallen to just 17,000 in 1997, and the majority of these were Bentleys. Other than a factory in Crewe with 2,500 employees and a reputation for excellent automotive hand-finishing, the business up for sale had few assets apart from its brands.

Rolls-Royce's destination was always likely to be Germany. BMW, which already supplied engines and parts for the cars, seemed the obvious destination. But the car manufacturer's final offer of £340 million ($568 million) was easily beaten by a bid from Volkswagen for £430 million ($718 million). But there was a legal wrinkle in the deal structure. The Rolls-Royce business had gained control of the brand name and the famous "RR" trademark when the aircraft engine and car businesses were split as part of a government nationalisation in 1971. Under that agreement, Rolls-Royce was not allowed to sell the name as part of any deal that included the car-manufacturing business.

Unfortunately, Volkswagen's lawyers did not know this. The German car manufacturer got all the IP rights to the cars themselves: the design rights of the luxury interior, the body and even the famous Spirit of Ecstasy hood ornaments. Effectively, it could build the cars but not advertise or sell them as Rolls-Royce. History does not record the reaction of Volkswagen's ambitious chairman, Ferdinand Piech, when he discovered the mistake, but a few expletives might have been exchanged. Matters got worse because BMW leveraged its close ties with Rolls-Royce to license the brand name from under Volkswagen's nose for just £40 million ($67 million).

However, the downward spiral did not stop there. BMW's contract to supply vital engines and components to Rolls-Royce – which were effectively just hand-finished in the UK – could be cancelled at 12 months' notice. Volkswagen did not have time to re-engineer the Rolls-Royce engine itself without taking production offline, so when BMW threatened to stop supply, it forced the clash between these close rivals to a head. The matter looked as though it was heading for court, but the German government intervened to push the two sides to arbitration.

Under the deal BMW would continue to supply engines for the cars and would let Volkswagen use the brand name from 1998 until 1 January 2003. From that date, only BMW would be able build cars bearing the Rolls-Royce name, and Volkswagen would be left building cars known as Bentleys. Effectively, BMW had bought Rolls-Royce for a tenth of the price paid by Volkswagen for Bentley, because it had done its legal homework.

Due diligence in cross-border M&A

The long-term trajectory of M&A activity is remorselessly upwards, despite temporary blips in the economic cycle. So is the trend for cross-border deals with international M&A activity growing even more quickly than domestic deals?

The background to this increased international activity is the growth of a global middle class, hungry for new products and services, as witnessed by Diageo's strategy for buying into the growing drinks market in Brazil and Turkey (see Chapter 2). Cross-border M&A growth is expected to continue over the long term. It is estimated that the global middle class will more than double in size from 2 billion today to 4.9 billion in 2030, according to the OECD. Driven by growth in China, India, Indonesia and Thailand, Asia is expected to host almost two-thirds of the global middle class by 2030 and account for 40% of global middle-class consumption, according to Reuters.

In countries in South America, and to a lesser extent Africa, M&A interest is shifting from natural resources and raw commodities to services such as health care and financial services, as well as luxury and near-luxury products. New commercial networks are emerging to serve M&A and expansion in fast-growing parts of the world, in particular a new "Silk Road", whereby south–south trade between Asian and South American countries bypasses Western commercial centres. Again, this can only bolster M&A growth.

Cross-border M&A, as with many topics in this book, could be the subject of a whole book, but it is worth considering a few of the basic principles for good practice:

■ Know your market. If you really understand your market, then it can't be "Europe" or "South America". Bolivia and Argentina, for example, share a border, but they are as different ethnically, culturally, geographically and linguistically as any two countries on the South American continent. Deal processes and legal systems are also not the same. Transpose that rule to Europe and the same could be said of Italy and Sweden or France and the UK. Local knowledge needs to be really local, certainly to a national level and sometimes even down to a region within a country.

■ Politicians are fickle and politics can derail a deal (Chapter 7 discusses the role that politics and regulation play in dealmaking). Any country has the potential to become interventionist under the right circumstances. After a long history of welcoming foreign investors, the US government blocked Dubai Ports World's rights to US ports that came under the company's control when it bought P&O, a UK ports operator. At the time, in 2006, the United Arab Emirates was one of the US's strongest Gulf allies, but public concerns about security in the wake of the 9/11 terrorist attacks in the US overrode all logical business and international relations arguments.

- Be prepared for longer, deeper due diligence. You may have to spend twice as much time and maybe money to get the same result as on a domestic deal.

- Choose the right cross-border partner. Diligent partner selection could be one of the most important factors in the success or failure of an international joint venture or strategic alliance (see Chapter 1). If you are going to do that to "get into a relationship", you'll certainly want to redouble your efforts if you are making the next step to propose a corporate marriage.

- Truly understand the people culture. As with M&A generally, it is easy to overlook the human component of any deal. Cultural nuances are crucial, both in completing the deal during the planning and negotiation process, and later when the deal needs to be implemented by the local team.

How long should due diligence take?

For a buyer seeking the right information about a target and its market, the answer to this question is: as long as it takes to get the answers. Even if you are doing a friendly deal where you have full access to the target and the deal has not yet been announced or has been leaked to the public, you need to find out where the right information resides and what it really means. You will, however, want to do this as quickly as possible because you are under significant time pressure to avoid competing bidders and the possibility that employees, clients and suppliers will leave the target.

As a general rule, large or financially complex target companies will require the most due diligence. Listed companies may want to limit what they make available because what is given to a friendly bidder must be shared with any rival bidders that may appear. But crucially, research demonstrates not only that longer due diligence results in a higher likelihood of success, but also that buyers do better the longer it takes, because this lowers the ultimate acquisition price.

When no one knows: pre-announcement M&A activity and its effect on M&A outcomes

There is a link between longer due diligence and the success of a deal as well as the payment of a lower premium, as found in research by Cass Business School's Mergers and Acquisitions Research Centre for Intralinks, a global technology provider of enterprise content collaboration solutions, conducted in 2013. The study was based on a sample of 519 publicly announced M&A transactions which used an Intralinks virtual data room (VDR) for due diligence between 2008 and 2012.

Although the link was a generally held truism, this was the first time its existence had been proven. The study found shareholder returns for acquirers to be significantly higher where due diligence was longer, with acquirers outperforming the market by 18.8% when they had a due diligence period longer than the average, compared with an underperformance of 6.7% for acquirers involved in deals with a shorter due diligence period.

There are sound reasons for this. Longer due diligence allows a buyer to dig deeper and find information about the target that it can use to negotiate harder on the price. However, the study provided anecdotal evidence from interviews with practitioners that indicates that there may be a limit to this advantage: even a friendly seller – particularly one that has other options – could become bored or insulted by too much due diligence and call time on a deal.

Sellers often try to limit the due diligence period for this reason, although their ability to do so depends on their power in the market and – particularly – the existence of rival bidders.

A. G. Barr's Irn Bru and Britvic's Indian Tonic Water taste very different, don't they?

Although a longer due diligence period may benefit buyers, giving them more time to unearth information they can use to negotiate a lower price for the target, there are times when an opportunistic buyer wants to prioritise a quick deal, either because a target is so distressed that it needs to be rescued, or because there is a one-off opportunity where the target, particularly a rival, is temporarily on the back foot.

Because the need for speed reduces the opportunity for long due diligence, outright "rescue" takeovers of insolvent or distressed companies are often low-cost and are the preserve of specialists. But the opportunity to buy a troubled rival or, from the perspective of a struggling business, the chance to attract a helpful industry partner can be too attractive for even the most cautious companies to pass up. In the heat of the pursuit, there is too great a temptation to bypass the due diligence basics outlined in this chapter, even in the traditional areas of legal and financial information that most firms insist on before a deal closes. And in the rush to complete a deal, it is easy to make mistakes in the people category of the three big mistakes of dealmaking, such as ill-thought-out decisions about the proposed partners' executive teams and their corporate culture.

Another argument against a longer due diligence process is the importance of maintaining the deal momentum. As shown in the case of the proposed merger between Britvic and A. G. Barr, two UK-based beverage companies, maintaining momentum and having all parties aligned is crucial if you want to reach a deal. As time moves on, even for just a few months, so do the industry dynamics and the need or want to sell or buy. In short, the deal may stall, but the rest of the world does not.

The answer of course is to have a clear, detailed checklist and process in place before commencing due diligence. In dealmaking situations you often hear about the 80/20 rule. There are the important aspects of due diligence, the 80%, which you need to fully understand and sign off on before a deal can be signed. The remaining 20% – often smaller issues that can take as long as the first 80% to get to the bottom of – are not deal-breakers, and buyers can take a punt on them when trying to close a deal quickly. Caution is needed, but with the right planning and significant pre-due diligence completed, this can be an effective deal strategy.

When trouble-hit Britvic announced in September 2012 that it was in £1.4 billion ($2.2 billion) merger talks with A. G. Barr, analysts cheered plans to create what was described in the deal announcement as "one of the leading soft drinks companies in Europe". For Britvic's shareholders, who had suffered a profit warning in 2011, its smaller listed rival looked like a cost-cutting knight in shining armour. Britvic's medium-term troubles had been significantly compounded by a forced safety recall of its child-focused Fruit Shoot drinks, which knocked 35% off its share price; combining with well-run A. G. Barr seemed like a solution to Britvic's financial woes and what the *Financial Times* described as its "highly leveraged" balance sheet.

A. G. Barr's shareholders, meanwhile, had seen their company shake off its sleepy image with fast-growing youth-focused drinks such as Rockstar and Irn Bru. What looked like a reverse takeover of a struggling larger rival, according to the *Daily Telegraph*, seemed an excellent and timely bit of business.

"The combination has compelling commercial and industrial logic," the parties said in their joint statement. In addition, they promised that a merged Britvic/A. G. Barr would deliver synergy savings of £40 million ($64 million) a year by 2016 and extend Britvic's strong relationships with the UK's biggest supermarket chains and its international partner and major shareholder, PepsiCo, to the rest of the business.

Few investors grumbled initially, but as the market digested the merger, some began to question its logic. In November 2012, an activist investor and Britvic's eighth-largest shareholder publicly criticised the deal as "poorly negotiated". The no-deal camp got more bad news when it emerged that A. G. Barr was to get half the seats on the combined board as well as the all-important chief executive role, which was to go to its highly respected chief executive, Roger White. Yet despite these challenges, only 6% of Britvic's shareholders ultimately voted against the deal.

The tie-up was made contingent on approval by the UK's entry-level competition authority, the Office of Fair Trading (OFT – whose functions have since been taken over by the Competition and Markets Authority or CMA), which clears a vast majority of mergers every year. As the deal lumbered through the UK's regulatory processes, no commentator predicted that the competition authorities would be a serious bar to a tie-up. After all, a combination of Britvic's orange-coloured Tango drink and A. G. Barr's Orangina was probably not uppermost in the government's mind when drawing up competition policy. Nevertheless, the competition authorities are a critical stakeholder for almost any deal – large or small – and neglecting to recognise this is dangerous.

So when in February 2013 the OFT referred the deal to the Competition Commission (now also superseded by the CMA) for a lengthy examination, there was much gnashing of teeth as Britvic and A. G. Barr complained that the market's dominant player, Coca-Cola, already had double their combined market share. Britvic's chairman, Gerald Corbett, was widely quoted as stating:

> If this is [UK] industrial policy, I am a Frenchman. This is about two British companies getting together to take on Coca-Cola. The winners today are cracking open bottles of champagne at Coca-Cola in Atlanta, Georgia.

Strip away the populist comments and the due diligence comes into question. Was a referral of the tie-up so unlikely that the companies – and their lawyers – should have made the deal contingent on quick approval by the OFT? For Britvic, which was dealing with the impact of the Fruit Shoot recall, it is clear that such a contingency was particularly palatable because only a quick tie-up would get it out of its immediate troubles. But from the perspective of A. G. Barr, which had been presented with the opportunity of a lifetime, it is hard to see why the company would choose to put a backstop on a merger unless its hand was forced.

The two sides promised to revisit the possibility of a merger following an investigation by the Competition Commission. Britvic's chief executive, Paul Moody, who had agreed to step down as part of the merger, was replaced in February 2013 by Simon Litherland, who had cut his teeth in the excellent Diageo team discussed in Chapter 2.

Litherland had been hired as Moody's successor before the A. G. Barr deal, so he was now in an unenviable position. But instead of sloping off into the sunset, he started a review to assess how he could improve Britvic's strategy regardless of any merger. He found £30 million ($47 million) a year of cost cuts that Britvic could implement itself; these had been overlooked when A. G. Barr's CEO had promised to find synergies of £40 million ($62 million) in a merged business. In announcing Britvic's rationalisation programme, he wiped out much of the financial rationale for a deal. Having recovered from the Fruit Shoot recall, Britvic's shares were now trading at nearly 500 pence per share and the company could renegotiate merger terms.

Once the Competition Commission cleared the deal in July 2013, Britvic tried to renegotiate its share of the merged company up from 63% to 70% and – crucially – it asked for control of the board of the new business, reputedly with Litherland replacing White as chief executive, according to reports in the *Daily Telegraph*. But their positions could not be reconciled and the two sides walked away, with A. G. Barr professing itself "disappointed" and Britvic lauding its former merger partners as "good people" but seeing a bright stand-alone future.

Several years later it looks as though someone at the OFT inadvertently did Britvic and its shareholders a favour in stalling the deal and allowing the company time to rethink its proposition. A. G. Barr's share price remained broadly undisturbed, while Britvic's shares hit a high in 2015 of 775 pence per share, almost three times higher than when the process started.

Successful due diligence has solid foundations

The building blocks of successful due diligence are solid corporate strategy and dedicated implementation of that strategy through continuous target selection. For example, Vista, a US private equity firm, paid more than its rivals to acquire Misys, a failing software business, but it had done enough homework to know that the target had more value than its competitors realised (this case is discussed in Chapter 4).

Financial sponsors, such as private equity firms that do more than 10–20 deals annually, are businesses that must – and do – excel at due diligence. An example is JAB Holding Company, a private investment company owned by the Reimann family, whose wealth dates back to the German Benckiser industrial chemicals business founded in the 1820s. It saw an undervalued gem in the Douwe Egberts coffee business in 2013 and, because JAB could see the opportunity it offered, it bought the coffeemaker ahead of rival bidders. In 2014 Douwe Egberts entered a joint venture with Mondelez, a global food conglomerate. At the end of 2015 JAB also purchased Keurig Green Mountain, a US coffee company, for $13.9 billion.

It is not just financial sponsors who are known for their excellent due diligence. Liberty Global, a US telecommunications and television company that was stalking ITV, a UK commercial broadcaster, in 2015, is known for its background research and speed, having completed the acquisitions of Virgin Media ($23.3 billion) and Ziggo ($13.7 billion) in record time in 2013 and 2014 in terms of starting the conversation/dialogue and completing the deal.

Getting it right the Cheung Kong Way

Cheung Kong Infrastructure (CKI) Holdings has been one of the most successful acquirers of the past decade. With an investment portfolio that spans Europe, Canada, Australia and New Zealand, the company's chairman is Victor Li, the eldest son of Sir Li Ka-shing, a global entrepreneur and Hong Kong's wealthiest citizen.

Like Diageo, CKI has a reputation for excellent target selection built on high-quality industry expertise. Putting in the homework early helps the company through the due diligence processes that are a crucial part of infrastructure asset auctions.

One of CKI's biggest European acquisitions was UK Power Networks, the non-core electricity distribution arm of EDF, a French power company that had penetrated the UK market with the purchase of several electricity companies, including London Electricity in 2002. EDF decided in 2010 that it wanted to be part of the UK's new nuclear-power programme, but it needed to divest assets to pay for that investment. Furthermore, returns in the electricity industry had been dampened by the 2009 recession and the industry also facing regulatory issues.

CKI, which had missed out on the earlier sale of a regional electricity distribution business, brought in Basil Scarsella, a long-term senior executive of the group, to run the bid, in conjunction with CKI's M&A executives, for the assets that would become UK Power Networks.

Scarsella believes that CKI's unique approach gives it an early advantage over other bidders, claiming:

CKI considers itself to be an operator of regulated assets, not just an investor ... CKI has owned and successfully operated regulated utilities assets in Hong Kong, Australia, United Kingdom, Canada and New

Zealand for a long time. When undertaking due diligence on possible acquisitions, CKI generally have a very good idea of areas in the business where they can add value.

This demonstrates another key point about due diligence done well: the need to know your own company's strengths and weaknesses in order to assess properly what complementary skills and resources are needed through a merger or acquisition.

The Hong Kong-based business does have a great reputation for bringing in good managers, applying best-in-class governance and then leaving them to run the business. In that sense it is sometimes viewed as an excellent hybrid – tying the interests of the company's backers to management's, but also having a corporate level of industry expertise.

Scarsella says that CKI's status as a long-term investor is also seen as a cornerstone of its success:

The proof is there for everyone to see that CKI is a long-term investor. Reputation is very important so CKI manages the businesses from a long-term perspective.

CKI has so far largely focused on developed markets where the state has already sold off most infrastructure assets. Given the size of the pool of potential investments, maintaining this reputation is a necessity, not a luxury.

From CKI in Asia to Rolls-Royce and Britvic in the UK, careful, holistic due diligence that takes into account issues such as cultural differences is vital. Adequate time must also be planned for this work: it cannot and should not be rushed.

This best-in-class due diligence is the building block not just for the next chapter on pricing but, if the deal does go through, for the post-deal period where excellent due diligence provides the foundation for excellent integration.

Knowledge is power: dos and don'ts

- ■ **Do** your homework; knowledge is power.
- ■ **Do** take your time – it might help reduce the price.

- **Don't** be afraid to move quickly if you need to as long as you have done the groundwork.

- **Don't** forget to consider carefully non-traditional risk factors such as culture, ethics and cyber-security in your due diligence process.

- **Don't** be afraid to walk away from a bad deal.

- **Do** remember to spend time on managing all the important stakeholders, as you will have to work together once the deal is done.

- **Don't** assume that you know everything about a target company, even if you think that you know the industry and the company well.

- **Do** conduct due diligence on your own company's capabilities to do the deal, including the integration.

4

Why the price isn't always right

CAST YOUR MIND BACK to the end of the last century when the Millennium bug was the world's biggest cyber-threat. The late 1990s and the millennial dotcom boom saw a slew of mega-deals that still dominate the M&A league tables. In 1999, the UK's Vodafone AirTouch launched an offer for its German rival Mannesmann in what remains the biggest-ever hostile cross-border bid. The deal was a totem of a telecoms boom that dwarfs the technology-market mania of the Facebook/WhatsApp age.

At the time, a captivated global business audience followed every twist and turn of a rare Anglo-American raid on a Germany company, until Mannesmann rolled over when Vodafone ultimately paid a massive $183 billion for a friendly merger. Approaching 20 years later, it remains the third-largest M&A deal ever.

Five years after the merger, Vodafone was forced to tell investors it was taking a £28 billion ($45 billion) "goodwill" charge, one of the biggest post-acquisitions write-downs on record. This was primarily due to the Mannesmann acquisition. Such a significant write-down of goodwill, defined as the difference between the net assets of an acquired business and the purchase price, indicated that Vodafone had mispriced its bid for Mannesmann.

Yet when the deal is considered – both at the time of the transaction and in the aftermath – pricing is low on the list of criticisms. This may sound surprising, but it is not. Pricing is not one of the fundamental three big mistakes of dealmaking – it is possible to pay a high price and still make the deal a success. Valuation and pricing – in contrast to the big three of planning, communication and people – are the one area of dealmaking where participants normally invest appropriate time and resources to it get right. Some firms do get it wrong (as did Vodafone), but typically it is something that gets appropriate attention.

The buyer's mechanism for determining the correct valuation – that is, its walkaway price – takes into consideration methods used by a wide variety of bidders from financial sponsors such as hedge funds, private equity firms and even sovereign wealth funds to strategic corporate acquirers, both private and public.

Many of the most obvious failures of valuation occur not because there is a mistake in the valuation methodology or process, but because a buyer's view on either the future forecasts or the risk, or both – and therefore inputs to its financial models – is inherently flawed.

A good example is the acquisition by Saudi Arabian investors of Continental Farmers Group, the owner of huge tracts of valuable fertile farmland in Ukraine. The Saudis bought the UK-listed agricultural business through an investment vehicle, United Farmers' Holding Company, as part of Saudi Arabia's strategic push for food security. The Saudi government, which has plenty of petrodollars but little arable land of its own, has in recent years encouraged state-backed companies to buy up farmland in Africa and near Asia.

Unfortunately, when Russia sent troops into separatist, ethnically Russian parts of eastern Ukraine in 2014, food production slowed and it became almost impossible to get food harvested and out of the country. Saudi Arabia's willingness to invest in unstable geopolitical regions – or certainly to do so for the £58 million ($88 million) it paid for the UK-listed company – was not primarily a valuation error or a due diligence mistake. Rather, it was a strategic gamble on a bad risk, or a mispricing of risk.

Valuation versus pricing

M&A valuation centres on striking a balance between the buyer's views of the value of the target and the "market", or the seller's expectations of the price to be paid (see Figure 4.1). To avoid overpayment, the bidder should always have established its walkaway price prior to embarking on potential target pursuit.

In summary, there are five steps to establishing a buyer's walkaway price – that is, the maximum price the buyer should be willing to pay.

FIGURE 4.1 **Valuation versus pricing**

Valuation
1 Target valuation assessment
2 Synergies
3 Costs and "business impact factor"

Pricing
1 Background – why sell?
2 Context – valuation of peers
and comparable transactions
3 Competition – quality of asset/interest
4 Negotiation tactics

Source: Authors

1 Stand-alone valuation to the equity shareholders

There are several different ways of doing this, including the target's financial performance in relation to the performance of comparable listed companies, assessing net asset value, or using management/ leveraged buy-out models determined by the company's financial forecast and the cost and availability of debt.

Many, if not all, valuation methodologies will be influenced by market or transaction multiples, that is, what other investors are prepared to pay for one unit (dollar, euro, pound, etc) of revenue or earnings of a company or its competitors. Public target bidders also need to consider the 52-week-high pre-bid target share price, as it has been shown to have an impact on the minimum bid level at which the shareholders are likely to accept an offer. In other words, each shareholder will have a view on the value of control, that is, the value of future benefits from the stock, and the memory of near-term historic valuations, which the premium paid has to exceed.

Interestingly, the average premium paid of 20–40% over the undisturbed share price in acquisitions of public targets has been remarkably consistent over time and across sectors, which is probably a reflection of the benchmark "value" of giving up control and future benefits for investors. These premiums vary by industry, country and point of time in the economic and M&A cycle.

2 Add: target's net debt

Enterprise value must consider the target's debt holders as well as shareholders. There will usually be a change-of-control clause in the debt holders' contract with the target company which means the acquirer will need to pay down or renegotiate that debt after the deal is completed.

Clearly, any outstanding cash belonging to the target can be used to net off the effect of the debt. This is why cash-rich companies are attractive acquisition targets.

3 Add: what is control of that business worth to my business?

This control allows the acquirer to achieve synergies. A synergy in this context is the notion that the two businesses are worth more together than as two separate entities. Synergies can be revenue- or cost-focused, with usually only the latter making it into models and deal communication, as it is relatively easier to control, measure and track. In some ways, synergies are also the inverse of the acquisition premium and should, at least in theory, ensure that the bidder with the greatest synergy potential prevails in an auction. However, for several reasons already discussed in this book – hubris, strategic mistakes, poor planning, external pressures, and so on – this is more easily promised than achieved. The value of acquisition synergies is also a key sweetener for investors in any share-based deal.

4 Do: valuation analysis

There is never a single, precise answer in M&A valuation. Scenario analyses and valuation ranges based on different possible outcomes are essential. With so many subjective and moving inputs, there simply is no such thing as the right M&A value, and all the values should be considered. This point is well demonstrated by the commonly used football field format, a given in any deal pitch-book (see Figure 4.2).

If a deal is agreed, the agreed price is likely to be somewhere between the low and the high end of the range, with the exact point being determined by non-financial factors such as the relative negotiation strength of the two parties.

FIGURE 4.2 **The valuation football field**

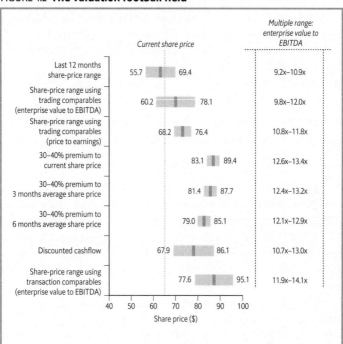

Source: Authors

5 Subtract: costs

These should include:

- Advisory costs – investment bankers, accountants, lawyers, public relations firms, stock agents, debt advisory fees, etc (these can be up to 5% of the negotiated deal price).

- Opportunity costs – what the company would be doing with the time and resources spent in the pre-completion phase if a deal was not being done (this is a difficult figure to estimate but should not be ignored for that reason, as it could be the highest individual deal-cost item).

- Dis-synergies – when the company is constrained to achieve certain cost synergies due to its size and scale in the market. This is particularly important if the buyer expects to have to divest assets as part of the deal, either to finance it or because of competition concerns.
- Integration costs – these can be up to 15% of the deal price, although spread out over several years.
- Funding costs (interest payments) – if bridge loans are required or if debt is being raised to purchase the target.

Clearly, there is an entire industry and many tomes devoted to discussing valuation methods. But despite their technical and apparently precise nature, the output should always be challenged on the basis of rationality and logic. Using valuation methods is an art, not a science, as will be made clear later in this chapter. Just because a complex valuation method spits out a result for the target's value does not mean that is the correct figure at the time of calculation, in that specific deal and for that buyer.

Having a formal process to determine the walkaway price, which, as with everything in M&A valuation, will be a range as opposed to a precise number, should help acquirers recognise and evaluate warning signs in the process when the negotiation is running hard. It should help executives provide a more objective justification to the buying company's board as to why it should make a decision to walk away. Finally, if an indication of price expectation has been given in an auction, it should help potential bidders determine early in the process if it is one in which they should participate.

Of course, the walkaway price only applies to the buyer's situation. Equally important is the selling shareholders' view on value, which will be crucial in the pricing.

There are five questions that will influence a "market" or the seller's view on pricing:

- Rationale – Why do I want or have to sell?
- Context – What have competitors sold for?
- Control – What premium will I, or my shareholders, accept for change of control?

- Competition – Can I get a higher bid from someone else?
- Finance – What can the bidder afford and can it borrow to pay more?

The most efficient buyers run valuation models alongside their live deal list and are often stricter in their approach to valuation: that is, they should have a view when it is time to walk away, or at least be more selective in the deal process they decide to participate in. The bid by the RBS-led consortium for ABN AMRO – a hurried deal with apparently little valuation planning and due diligence – is the counterpoint to that approach. CEOs who have not put in their early groundwork will find it much harder to pull out later because at that point they and their team (including the board of directors) will be influenced by other factors. These include emotional ties to the deal: there is often a tendency to assume the target will be won and to attribute significance to the sunk costs of both time and money already invested in the deal process.

Because of this overconfidence, managers who are responsible for their company's M&A process, and have a successful track record on past deals, are more likely to embark on a "riskier" strategy. This could include cross-border transactions, which may require regulatory approval in multiple jurisdictions, or hostile takeovers.

Masters of the deal

Despite our claim that a high price does not necessarily mean a disastrous deal, there is evidence that successful dealmakers are price-savvy and are better at "timing the market". Indeed, they are more likely to strike when others are encumbered, when a target can be bought for a much lower price.

According to global research conducted in 2015 by Intralinks and Cass Business School, *Masters of the Deal: Part 2*, more successful M&A corporates – measured by share-price value generated after the acquisition(s) or divestiture(s) – significantly increase their deal-value ratio of divestments to acquisitions in times when markets are hot and crucially valuations are high. Similarly, they shift their ratio towards more acquisitions than divestments when markets are less inflated.

FIGURE 4.3 **Buy and sell patterns of successful dealmakers**

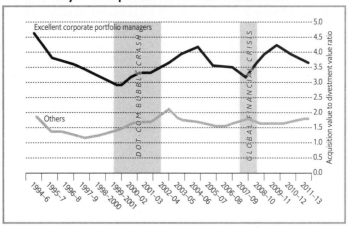

Source: *Masters of the Deal, Part 2*, Intralinks, 2015

In our experience, the advantages for successful buyers also include a strong corporate culture and good preparation, through both solid long-term implementation of deal strategy and effective due diligence.

Overpaying isn't the end of the world

One company that proves that second chances do exist is Misys, a software provider that went from an unloved public company to a takeover target in an overpriced private equity transaction. The company's owner, Vista, won a bidding war to get Misys, but paying over the odds has not held it back.

In 2012, Misys was listed on the London Stock Exchange. It was overleveraged and undermarketed, and its shareholders were mutinying. The company's client base then, as now, comprised principally large international banks and financial institutions which were struggling through a euro-zone crisis that considerably weakened their willingness to invest in software.

It looked as though things were getting worse as Misys reported a 12% fall in revenues to £89 million ($143 million) for the third quarter of 2012. The company's shareholders – pension funds as well as hedge funds and other activists – were unwilling to wait years for things to get better, so they supported the sale of the company, basically to anyone who would have it and would be willing pay a reasonable price. They were not greedy.

With their shares worth just 260 pence each, investors were particularly annoyed that a deal to sell Misys to a US buyer in 2011 for 450 pence a share had fallen through. It looked as if they would now have to accept an all-share bid from a Swiss trade rival, Temenos, without a premium to the share price – an unusual situation, as most offers for public targets include the aforementioned 20–40% control premium. However, Misys and its investment bankers managed to get a bidding war going.

CVC, a private equity firm, and Value Act, Misys's biggest investor, holding 21.5% of the company, seemed to be carrying the day with a higher bid. But another private equity firm, US-based Vista, got Misys's non-executive directors on side and made a surprising 350 pence a share bid at a 6% premium to the company's share price, which had already been bumped up by CVC's bid.

Vista, a technology specialist, ended up valuing Misys at more than £1.2 billion ($2 billion), even though its revenues were falling. Analysts described Vista's price as "full" and many commentators thought the private equity firm had paid a big premium that was artificially pushed up by a bidding war.

But so far Vista has made a huge success of Misys, combining it with one of its portfolio companies, Turaz, a former Thomson Reuters business that provides software for managing treasury and capital-market transactions. Then it bolted on IND, a mobile-banking software provider, and Custom Credit Solutions, which makes software for managing the loan-origination process.

Vista brought in Nadeem Syad, an Oracle veteran with whom it had worked before, who – thanks in part to an improvement in European financial markets – turned Misys around. At the end of 2014, Vista appointed investment banking advisers to prepare the company for a dual-track process (sale or IPO) and, according to Sky News, then had talks with a number of parties including Temasek, Singapore's sovereign wealth fund.

What is most likely is that Vista knew and understood the potential for Misys better than anyone else, so it could afford to pay more than others (overpaying, in the eyes of those competitors) because it could extract more value from the business. Vista had done its due diligence, which was then reflected in the deal valuation, and thus was willing to pay a higher price.

It is not surprising that a study by *Forbes* magazine of 500 chief financial officers who had been involved in a merger puts overpayment low on the list of why deals fail. Overpayment is seventh, below incompatible cultures, an inability to manage the target and a clash of management styles – all of which belong in the "failure to properly consider people" big mistake. Also rated as a bigger problem than overpayment was a failure to anticipate foreseeable events, as happened with the global mining sector around 2007 and the Saudi Arabian farmland investors in Ukraine, even though in both of these examples there was evidence at the time of the possibility of a change in market circumstances.

Pricing in risk

Failing to anticipate foreseeable events is ultimately a failure to assess underlying strategy. With the Ukrainian farmland deal, priced at a 48% premium to the undisturbed share price despite falling earnings for the target company, it certainly seemed that the Saudi Arabian investors had a fundamentally different view (in hindsight too low) on the appropriate risk than the rest of the market. Given that the Caucasus region has a long-standing history of Russian support for separatist, ethnically Russian people in former Soviet countries, that risk should have been better anticipated in their valuation calculations.

Sometimes events that could have a huge impact on takeovers are not foreseeable (so-called "black swan" events), but rarely do they come completely without warning. There are well-developed processes in risk management for identifying possible (but not necessarily probable) scenarios, and the pricing and valuation calculations for an M&A deal should be stress-tested through these scenarios.

Deals hit by potentially foreseeable changes in technology include the disastrous AOL/Time Warner merger, which failed to anticipate the massive shift fast internet would create in the entertainment market, even though there were definite signs that this was the way things were moving at the time of the merger. A number of well-known analysts were saying at the time that they could not understand the deal. Tom Wolzien, a stock analyst at Sanford C. Bernstein, was reported by the *New York Times* shortly after the deal was announced as saying that "there's a real difficult time with the Street by and large coming to grips with the combination", and that neither AOL nor Time Warner were easy to understand because AOL got its revenue from subscriptions, advertising and internet commerce, whereas Time Warner had five major divisions, each with its own different business cycle.

The effects of regulatory reform should also be anticipated. For example, financial regulation that bans payment-protection insurance or a medical regulator banning a pharmaceutical company from making a particular medicine are risks that are foreseeable. However, few blind spots have been as obvious as the one that developed among executives in the mining industry in 2007.

With the world on a rapid upward economic trajectory, the years that led up to the 2008 financial collapse were good ones for most commodities. Not only were the US and Europe booming, but the fast-growing BRICs also were joining the party. China and India were building new cities at a pace the miners could not match and commodity prices soared as they fought with Latin American buyers over aluminium and iron ore.

The emerging-markets boom convinced Big Mining – including Rio Tinto's chief executive, Tom Albanese – that the industry had entered a new super-cycle where there would be no slowdown. Ever.

This cloak of invincibility gave Albanese and Rio Tinto's biggest rivals – BHP Billiton, Glencore and Xstrata – the confidence to go on spending sprees. The term super-cycle was still being used in 2009 as western European and US banks begged for taxpayer bail-outs, but Albanese did not acknowledge the new reality – the need for less aluminium and iron as car production, heavy machinery and building works slowed down – until 2013, when he was pushed out in the wake of a \$38 billion write-down.

Albanese had joined Rio Tinto in 2007 at the top of the cyclical commodities peak when aluminium prices were at a 20-year high. At the same time as the world's biggest aluminium producer, Alcan, wanted protection from an unwanted bidder, Albanese's company was being pursued by its own unfriendly bidder, BHP Billiton. Sealing the deal for $38.1 billion – a 65% premium on Alcan's undisturbed share price – was, Albanese claimed, "a case of being in the right place at the right time".

Alcan's former chief executive, Dick Evans, describes it rather differently. Talking to the *Wall Street Journal* in 2013 with the benefit of hindsight, he called it "one of the worst decisions ever, the largest metals and mining transaction in the history of the world at the high point of the commodity cycle".

Buying Alcan did help Rio Tinto to fend off the unfriendly approach from BHP Billiton, although by the time its rival formally abandoned the chase it was November 2008 – and two months after the collapse of Lehman Brothers it would have been hard for BHP Billiton to borrow money for the deal. Regulators had also threatened to tie the deal up in months of red tape.

The Alcan deal, meanwhile, left Rio Tinto highly overleveraged just as the world was heading into the financial crisis; overnight, the company's net debt increased to $46.3 billion, or 94.5% of turnover, from $2.4 billion, or 9.4% of turnover.

Rio Tinto was not the only miner to gorge on spare cash generated by the commodities boom. Brazil's Vale bought Inco for $18 billion in 2006 and America's Freeport-McMoRan Copper & Gold Inc bought Phelps Dodge for $23 billion.

The world's largest mining groups have written off about 90% of the value of their M&A deals completed since 2007, according to a report by Citibank in 2015. The bank calculates that, overall, miners built up impaired assets worth $85 billion in those seven years, representing 18% of their average asset base. Most affected were Rio Tinto, which had 34% of its asset base impaired, and Anglo American, with 23% impairment.

Rio Tinto did the biggest deal at the worst possible time. One of the large credit-rating agencies, Fitch, said it was concerned that it might need to lower the company's credit rating. Rio Tinto was forced to go cap in hand to shareholders for a rescue rights issue, and was then left trying to sell assets to streamline itself at a time when there were few buyers for anything, and even fewer who could afford it.

As the economy improved slowly, Rio Tinto hung on, hoping

that aluminium prices would pick up. But it had misread China, underestimating that country's growing domestic aluminium output and overestimating demand for the metal, which was constrained by a fall in sales of new cars.

The company delayed write-downs, taking only $1 billion in 2009 against the Alcan purchase. But when the hoped-for bounce failed to come, it was forced to write down a further $14 billion against both that deal and a $3.9 billion Mozambican coal acquisition personally spearheaded by Albanese in 2011.

At this point Albanese's position was no longer tenable. He said in his farewell statement in January 2013:

> While I leave the business in good shape in many respects, I fully recognise that accountability for all aspects of the business rests with the CEO.

Valuing intangibles

As well as strategic errors in judgment that lead buyers to misprice risk, there is also a category of "true" pricing errors where a buyer has attached a value to a target's asset, but has under- or overvalued it, or – even more worryingly – not recognised it as an asset.

It is hard to imagine that despite the value in most businesses nowadays being derived from intangible sources, these are neither identified nor audited in financial statements. It is only in M&A transactions that they appear on the books, and even in a transaction situation the allocation of purchase price will ascribe value to those easy-to-identify intangibles such as registered IP rights but then gather most of the value together in one word: goodwill. For reasons that should become apparent, we predict the death of goodwill, at least in accounting terms.

In a world driven and dominated by disruptive technologies, careful assessment of truly valuable but more or less identifiable assets and intangible IP is an increasingly important issue in M&A. Badly managed in a transaction, IP can be a quagmire that can adversely effect any M&A deal, as Volkswagen found when it acquired Rolls-Royce only to discover it had not bought the rights to use the luxury carmaker's name (see Chapter 3). Volkswagen's error is not a one-off: equally famously eBay bought Skype for $3.2 billion and seemed not to recognise that the core Skype technology relied on a licence from an entity outside the transaction perimeter which then expired after the purchase.

In the past, IP evaluation has been limited to "black-letter" registered IP rights, that is, patents (particularly important in the life sciences industry), trademarks, design rights, domain names and copyrights.

Because of this, IP due diligence has traditionally been carried out by law firms. During the due diligence phase they focus on the IP that can be easily seen and therefore assessed and will typically:

- ensure the target owns or has the right to use the registered IP that comprises part of the sale (in an assets sale) or is owned by the target (in a share sale) and verify, quantitatively, that this registered IP exists;

- check the impact of change of control on the registered IP;

- establish whether there are any pending legal challenges to the target's registered IP or infringements of third-party registered IP rights by the target and aim to establish the risk in both cases;

- negotiate warranties from the seller to confirm the above – sometimes this will be done instead of due diligence rather than in addition to it.

The buyer and its advisers will seek to value the assets acquired and allocate value between the tangible and intangible assets acquired.

Valuation of IP is normally carried out post-sale using one of the three main methods:

- **Cost.** What would it cost to replace the IP asset based on benchmark figures? The challenge here is that benchmarks are not always available and, even where a buyer or adviser suggests that they are, upon further due diligence the IP assets are often found to be unique in ways that make benchmarks difficult to use as accurate comparables.

- **Market.** How much would it cost to buy a similar asset? Similar to the issue of benchmarking availability, the uniqueness of both IP assets and individual M&A deals can make it difficult to identify a similar asset and determine its value.

■ **Income.** How much revenue will the asset provide once it is owned? This calculation can be based on the alternative cost of licensing the IP from a third party or on an estimate of the additional profits generated by the target business compared with the profits of that business without the IP. This income estimate can then be projected for, say, the next 5–10 years and, using net present value calculation techniques, modelled to determine a current value for the revenue stream.

In recent years, however, there has been an acceptance that there is significant value in other intangibles that extend beyond the scope of legal IP due diligence.

Andrew Watson, head of IP strategy at EY, an international accountancy and professional-services firm, says:

> The main challenges with intangibles and IP are that there is no consistent lens used to assess which intangibles are the most important sources of value and no common language in which to talk about them. It is typical to find that after the value of tangible assets of the target are deducted from the purchase price, as much as 95% of the value will be intangible. Take off the value of the registered IP rights using a method such as relief from royalty and there is still a large amount of value that will typically be allocated to "goodwill". If a buyer does not have an appreciation of all of the assets being acquired and legal diligence does not, in fact could not, identify and assess them, there has to be a serious risk of impairment to goodwill.

Within this goodwill element are many assets of different shapes and sizes. A company's people – executives and staff – are the main repositories of that intangible value. The most valuable asset of most companies is the knowledge of what to do and, indeed, what not to do (a right known as negative know-how); expertise on how to build or take a product to market on the one hand and supplier relationships on the other are other examples of this. Rarely can such knowledge be underpinned by formal legal IP rights such as patent or trademark protection. Indeed, a well-thought-through IP strategy would deliberately decide not to apply for registered protection of these assets.

The main exception to the rule that most value is in the unregistered

IP rights is in the life sciences sector. In pharmaceuticals, most of the intangible value is in the patents, which give a right to exclude a competitor from using the same invention for 20 years. The patent cliff will apply at the end of the patent life, at which point 80% of the revenues will typically disappear within two weeks and never come back. However, even in this sector, there are other high-value intangibles such as expertise in compliance with regulatory approvals and R&D collaborations.

In terms of the three big mistakes of dealmaking, valuation mistakes are often fundamentally people mistakes. If staff and executives hold the keys to intangible value that is not underpinned by formal IP rights, a buyer should find ways within the transaction structure both to unlock and to transfer that value and encourage the holders to stay. Buyers must be careful to ensure that where they think they see no value in an incumbent management team, the intangible value of the company resides elsewhere in the company, for instance in lower-level managers or groups of staff such as R&D or marketing teams. The key, first, is to identify and evaluate the asset base. How to deal with this in the transaction context will depend on the nature of the specific asset.

Even when a buyer does put a value on the senior-management team, it may often not do enough to persuade them to stay with the business post-deal completion. An example is HP's acquisition of Autonomy in 2011 (see Introduction). At $11 billion, or 24 times EBITDA, HP's valuation of Autonomy was a stretch by any definition. At the time of the purchase it was widely believed that HP wanted Autonomy not just for its software but also for its dynamic management team, led by serial technology entrepreneur and founder Mike Lynch. The desire to keep the management on board was believed to be a key reason for HP's willingness to pay a full price.

This made sense because Lynch and the Autonomy senior-management team were repositories of much of the intangible and therefore total value of the company. It was objectively clear and would make IP strategic sense for Autonomy's IDOL search technology to be protected not by patents but by trade secrets. (Why would someone patent and therefore make publicly available a search technology when it could not ever discover infringement by a third party?) It is likely that when HP conducted its IP diligence it analysed Autonomy's patents and other registered rights. But, as with a growing number of new technology businesses, Autonomy's IP value was not just in its patents but also in its trade secrets – apparently around 600 of them. And who has access to trade secrets in a company? The senior-management team, of course.

IP due diligence

Specialist teams at advisory firms have been identifying these trends and beginning to fill this gap. Rather than replacing the traditional law firm due diligence, these advisers work alongside the lawyers performing qualitative due diligence on IP and intangible assets to back up the legal due diligence.

EY's Andrew Watson, who has also previously worked as an M&A lawyer, has created what he calls a "universal taxonomy of intangibles". This is used to help buyers identify all intangibles and then, using an associated methodology, establish which are the most important in driving value. This analysis feeds into the valuation exercise required. Watson says:

> We place a lens over a business to work out what is really at the source of value. Outside of life sciences most companies could lose most of their patents and it would make little difference to its success. We need to look outside of the registered rights using a new lens to find that value. Often it may be a team of highly regarded men in white coats (literally) who are able to design products to meet the requirements of the future product roadmap.

The system was created with data from over 300 projects where the commercial value of IP was assessed. Watson and his team built this into a benchmarking system for intangibles, and the core data is constantly augmented. As Watson says, "this is a brave new world".

Another example is Microsoft, a company that changed the computing world with its Windows software. It has not had a happy time in the M&A market. Before its $26.2 billion offer in mid-2016 for LinkedIn, one of its biggest deals – and the largest in terms of people and plant – was its acquisition of the handset division of Finland-based Nokia, another once-great tech giant on the slide.

In 2013, Steve Ballmer, the same CEO who dallied with Yahoo!, decided that Microsoft had to get into the mobile-phone business, which was fast becoming the principal technology people were using to access the internet. A deal to buy Nokia's handset business for $7.9 billion closed in April 2014, but just 15 months later Ballmer's successor, Satya Nadella, announced a $7.6 billion write-down of Nokia's assets and axed 7,800 staff from the company. That is $7.3 billion written off in just over a year.

In the years leading up to the deal, Microsoft and Nokia were both victims – to a greater or lesser degree – of all-conquering tech giants Google and Apple. Nokia had been hit much harder. With its business squeezed between Apple's iPhones and rivals who ran Google's Android on their handsets, the Finnish business was losing money as it stuck by a deal with Microsoft to use its once dominant Windows operating system on its mobile devices.

Microsoft's performance had been better than Nokia's thanks to its Windows computer software, which, although it had lost ground to Apple products in home computing, had held up in the business market. But in the long term, Microsoft saw its future threatened by the increasing demands of customers for synchronised information on all their devices. The company knew that people wanted to be able to start an e-mail on their laptop and finish it on their phone, and Microsoft would only be in the game if people bought Windows-based handsets.

In the wake of rumours that Nokia was about to ditch Windows in favour of the more widely used Google-developed Android operating system, Ballmer announced the acquisition of Nokia. The problem was that by the time he made his decision the ship had well and truly sailed. Few consumers wanted a Windows-based phone; just 3% of mobiles globally used the operating system. Microsoft had totally misunderstood the value of the Nokia handset business to its overall empire and bought something that was nearly worthless.

The acquisition was bad news for both sides. Microsoft said that it would concentrate on its core business customers, leading many analysts to ask why it didn't buy BlackBerry, the businessperson's favourite mobile phone at the time, instead of Nokia. The company has also concentrated on developing holovision eyewear and other devices it hoped would make handheld phones redundant in a generation. Embattled Nokia, meanwhile, did get some cash for its shareholders, but many of the job cuts were made in Nokia's Finnish plants, causing an outcry in Norway where the mobile-phone pioneer was once a national champion and, according to *The Economist*, contributed a quarter of Finnish growth from 1998 to 2007.

Deals leak

Research shows that the longer due diligence goes on, the lower an offer price is likely to be (see Chapter 3). A seller's best option to limit due diligence is to orchestrate a competitive bid process from the outset. Another pricing tactic – albeit not as openly discussed – is to leak news of the deal.

When No One Knows, a November 2013 study on pre-announcement M&A activity by Cass Business School and Intralinks, found evidence to suggest that many, if not most, deal leaks are deliberate. The research data suggested that there is no corollary between a specific event, such as the opening of a deal-room or the hiring of advisers, and the timing of leaks. Instead, they tend to appear towards the end of the process and are likely to be motivated by one party being unhappy with how negotiations are progressing. Information is therefore leaked to push the deal in the preferred direction. In our experience, even if the leak itself is not deliberate, the target deal team's decision on whether to confirm the deal talks "off the record" can be.

In a related annual study of leaks, Intralinks and Cass found a drop in the number of deals showing suspicious trading activity before the deal announcement from approximately 14% of all public deals in 2008 to 6% in 2014. Notably, through most of that period, leaks are more common in Europe and the Middle East than in the US, perhaps because of greater enforcement of rules prohibiting leaks in the US through much of that period.

A leak has advantageous consequences for valuation because it may start the clock on formal takeover rules, if any, thereby putting pressure on buyers. It also flushes out potential counter-bidders. Even the whisper of a counter-bid might be enough to encourage a confirmed buyer to move more quickly, perhaps short-cutting the due diligence process that could uncover additional information about the target.

It is not difficult to see why leaks are part of the deal tactic toolbox. The annual study on leaks found that leaked deals deliver on average a significant increase in takeover premium of 18%.

How to pay

Most buyers will have a broad idea of how they plan to finance a takeover by the time they get to the valuation phase. But it is only after a buyer has ascribed a final price to pay that the fine details can be filled in.

In the private sphere and in small and medium-sized companies, especially family-owned ones, most takeovers are paid for in cash, funded by existing funds, debt or a combination of these. In the listed world of large global corporations, it is possible to make a "stock-financed" offer where the buyer pays solely with its own shares, although in practice most takeovers are funded with an element of cash.

A company's individual circumstances, the logistics of the deal and its appetite for risk will influence the proportional mix of funding. Specifically, management and its advisers will consider:

- the details of the transaction, including the financial and dilution impact on its existing equity shareholders, earnings and share price;
- the deal's impact on the company's financial stability and security, assessing the long-term impact of financing on its income statement, cash flow and balance sheet, including the ability to refinance the debt;
- how important it is to get the deal done quickly and confidentially, as cash deals can usually be faster than share or complex hybrid deals.

Of course, all are strongly influenced by the negotiation process in terms of what the seller will accept or believes the shareholders will accept.

When a company wants to include an element of cash in the acquisition price, and it is not using existing funds available on the balance sheet, it has broadly the following options:

- A listed company can issue new equity to existing shareholders or place equity with new shareholders. If a company is private, it might even go public to raise cash for acquisitions. Facebook, for example, bought WhatsApp in 2014 for $19 billion shortly after going public itself, paying a significant portion in cash.

- Sell corporate bonds or take on new debt from a bank or other lender.

- Sell a piece of the existing business to help fund the acquisition. An example is Diageo, which disposed of its non-core food assets, such as Burger King, to fund an acquisition spree. But the disposal does not have to take place before the purchase of the new company, as buyers can use bridging finance for the initial acquisition with a plan (or even a formal agreement already in place) to sell off non-core assets after the deal is completed. For example, Glencore, a commodities and trading company, sold off Dakota Growers Pasta, a pasta-making business, soon after its takeover of Xstrata.

Sometimes payment can be staggered, deferred or linked to performance criteria. This is a common technique for small and medium-sized businesses that are growing quickly. The acquirer will seek to de-risk the purchase price by linking future growth to the payment terms. The price paid can also include a lock-in element for key management and staff that encourages them to stay by prohibiting them from working for a competitor for a period of time, typically two years. One problem with linked payments is that true integration is then somewhat limited. This is why it is used more widely in strategic bolt-on acquisitions or private-equity-backed transactions (see the case of Mergermarket Group in Chapter 9).

In some instances, a seller can provide its own financing for a purchaser. This is especially common in financial services where banks selling off their divisions in the wake of the financial collapse provided so-called "stapled" finance to prospective buyers, whereby the financing and sale were part of the same deal – "stapled together".

Tax, the economic climate and changing investment practices have also had a huge influence on M&A deal financing. In the 1980s cash was king. In the 1990s there were mega-deals, such as when BP, a large UK-based oil company, purchased Amoco, an Illinois-based oil company, with shares. In the run-up to the global economic collapse, the easy availability of cheap debt meant share deals were rare; and when the money supply dramatically tightened after 2008, stock-financed (equity only) deals were suddenly back in vogue.

Stock-financed offers can allow a bidder more flexibility in a hostile situation because – as long as the share-exchange ratio is skewed to the buyer's advantage – such approaches are relatively low-risk (see Chapter 5).

Acquisitions that are funded principally by shares are more likely to be timed, that is, announced at a time when the bidder's shares are considered to be highly or fairly valued. There is a belief among some experts that takeover bids using equity destroy value for shareholders, which is confirmed in numerous studies from the 1990s and early 2000s. Warren Buffett, an investor in Kraft, publicly advised the food group's CEO, Irene Rosenfeld, that she was using too much of what he considered to be Kraft's undervalued stock in its 2009 bid for Cadbury.

However, a 2015 study challenges the conventional wisdom regarding the impact of funding in acquisition success. Crucially, it found not only that share-financed acquisitions are not value-destructive, but also that the type of funding used for a takeover generally makes no difference to its financial success or failure. *Do Stock-Financed Acquisitions Destroy Value? New Methods and Evidence* by three academics, Andrey Golubov, Dimitris Petmezas and Nickolaos Travlos, found no evidence for the overvalued equity hypothesis:

> *Stock-financed acquisitions are not value destructive and the method of payment generally has no further explanatory power in the cross section of acquirer returns.*

No doubt the topic of valuation in M&A will continue be a focus for professionals, and rightly so. With changing industry dynamics and the upward trend in dealmaking, in terms of both the number of deals and aggregate value, there will be new tools for valuation and new and innovative ideas for deal financing. Valuation and pricing in this context will continue to be debated – and this is what enables deals to happen. In other words, the (positive) valuation gap between the buyer and the seller is what creates the market, and although they use the same or similar methods and models to get there, inputs, forecasts and expectations will differ, hence our belief that there is no such thing as the right price.

Valuation gaps can be bridged by other levers, such as speed to completion, deal terms and financing. That the highest bidder does not always win the target is not unheard of. Money, it appears, is not always everything. And although risks can equal rewards, the analyses supporting those calculations must be backed up by exhaustive due diligence, examining both the target company and external factors such as disruptive technologies, market trends, likely competitive responses and, where necessary, socioeconomic factors.

With all these moving and subjective parts, paying a price above market expectations does not need to be fatal for the outcome of a deal, as long as the big three mistakes of dealmaking are carefully considered, although the job is certainly made easier by not overpaying.

Why the price isn't always right: dos and don'ts

- **Do** carefully consider your walkaway price, and be willing and prepared to walk.
- **Do** link your due diligence with your valuation, including for the difficult-to-value intangibles.
- **Don't** let the other side be better prepared.
- **Don't** pay out all your synergies by offering too high a premium.
- **Don't** forget to consider all the costs associated with the deal.
- **Do** plan for the financing of the deal early and spend time striking acceptable terms for both the buyer and seller.
- **Do** remember that overpaying is not necessarily an insurmountable obstacle, but it can make the ultimate success of the deal more difficult.
- **Don't** forget that M&A valuation is an art not a science: values and pricing differ in each deal.

PART 2

The deal

5

Negotiating tactics

IF YOU WERE WATCHING the 1987 film *Wall Street* – or any other Hollywood movie about a corporate takeover, actual or imaginary – the deal-negotiation phase would come near the start. For non-business readers, this chapter is where this book should begin.

In the real world, four chapters of strategy, planning, due diligence and valuation are needed to get to this point in the deal. In this chapter the groundwork on long-term strategy and target selection (discussed in Chapters 1 and 2), combined with the heavy lifting on due diligence and valuation (from Chapters 3 and 4), finally starts to pay off. Of the three big mistakes of dealmaking, it is the people and planning categories that are tackled in this chapter.

The single factor that distinguishes the best buyers from the rest is their willingness to invest large amounts of leadership time, money and organisational focus in a deal. What that buys is knowledge and expertise. The old adage that knowledge is power has never been truer than in M&A – and in this chapter. This is also true for the management team and shareholders on the sell side of the deal: for selling shareholders and management teams, the single best indicator of the seriousness of the buyer is the involvement of senior management on the bidder side.

One deal – Malcolm Glazer's acquisition of Manchester United Football Club in 2005 – showcases this principle perfectly. But as Microsoft's failed bid for Yahoo! in 2008 shows, the most intimate industry knowledge will not deliver if the negotiation tactics are wrong.

Every deal is unique. Even the best negotiating tactics are non-transferable: the blitzkrieg shareholder offensive used successfully by Shire in its all-share pursuit of Baxalta would not, for instance, have worked for Glazer's all-cash leveraged buy-out of Manchester United. Indeed, Glazer's strategy to buy Manchester United was very different from the way he negotiated and purchased the US Tampa Bay Buccaneers football team years earlier.

Given the specificity of every deal, there is little point in having a fully worked M&A playbook. Basic principles that can be applied to each individual deal are much better, but awareness of the options available remains critical and is covered here.

Friend or foe?

The starting point for any negotiating strategy is to determine whether a deal is friendly. Because unfriendly approaches of public companies dominate the headlines, it is easy to forget that 97% of M&A deals start by mutual consent. Assuming you are operating in that overwhelmingly friendly majority, the skeleton approach should be to:

- clarify where the two parties stand;
- identify resistance points;
- find zones of agreement;
- determine the best possible solution for both parties, creating a win–win.

Auctions: does the highest bidder always win?

Many sellers, particularly since the arrival in force of financial sponsors such as hedge funds and private equity firms, conduct their disposals or whole company sales by auction. Therefore, it is worth making a few general points here about the auction process and bidders' reputations.

An auction may seem like a cut-and-dried financial mechanism, but the following should guide a seller's choice of buyer:

- How successful have the buyer's previous deals been?
- What is the buyer's history in dealing with target managements?
- Are there many issues on which the buyer and seller are likely to take different positions?

- Has the buyer backed out of previous deals, either entirely or to renegotiate significant points?
- How involved and visible are senior and key decision-makers?
- Does the buyer have access to sufficient financing?

As this checklist shows, sellers evaluate bidders' approaches and abilities in dealmaking. Therefore acquirers need to be mindful of their reputation, especially private equity buyers who regularly participate in auctions. As in the sale of Mergermarket Group, an auction that attracted 50 interested parties in the first round, gaining a competitive advantage through more than a formal, written submitted bid can prove crucial (see Chapter 9).

Although a longer due diligence process is positive for the buyer, as it could give it more ammunition to negotiate down the purchase price, this is a less than ideal scenario for everyone. The better option is for bidders to have done significant research and to be given access to enough information pre-bid to provide a bid that they can stick closely to throughout the negotiation process.

For the seller, if its business is in order, the financials stack up, and there are no skeletons in the closet, there should be no reason to give away any discount in pricing or terms. This way, the final price should and possibly will match the initial expectations, pleasing the seller and making its acceptance of the offer more likely. Similarly, the bidder will win the prize without getting a reputation for a negotiation strategy that appears to outsiders to be continually chipping away at the price.

In the small percentage of situations that are not friendly – that is, the 3% that start off unsolicited (although less than 1% of deals end up without a recommendation to sell from the target's board) – the negotiating strategy will be determined by a range of issues, including the following:

- What you want to do with the company.
- How much – and how – you are paying for it.
- The stance of the target's board and that of its investors (these may differ).
- Whether the company has any other alternatives, as a desperate seller is very different from a reluctant one.

■ Whether the company has any defensive anti-takeover protections to defer bidders or make a hostile purchase unreasonably expensive (some of these are called poison pills when particularly offensive to any bidder).

For instance, if the buyer needs to persuade the target's board to recommend the bid, it will take a conciliatory approach; if it takes a hostile approach, it will ignore the board's resistance, go around them directly to the shareholders to get their approval, and then ultimately sack the board once the deal is done.

It is not just about shareholder approval, however, as the buyer needs to consider how to pay for the target. The main reason truly hostile bids – that is, those made via a formal offer to shareholders in the face of stated board opposition – are so rare, is that lenders will often not back them. A listed company making a share-based offer has much more freedom in this regard than a financial sponsor or private company that has only cash to offer.

It is not uncommon for private companies to offer themselves for sale but at the same time prepare for a public listing. This is known as a dual-track process and the two different outcomes compete with each other, as we saw in Chapter 4 with Vista/Misys.

In this context, most so-called hostile bids are actually "bear hugs" – a mechanism whereby bidders bypass the board initially and target investors directly with attractive offers (the hug), usually with an offer premium that is above the industry average. No serious bidder will take this route unless it has the funds – and the will – to bring shareholders round though a combination of charm, logic and cash, plus a threat and ultimately a willingness to go hostile as a last resort.

Hard or soft?

The style of the negotiations as opposed to the substance of the approach is often determined by the advisers – lawyers, accountants, PR firms and investment bankers – which usually take the lead.

Good-quality advice is crucial. An independent series of studies between 2013 and 2015 by academics at the University of Surrey and New York University's Stern School of Business found that companies represented by the world's largest multinational investment banks and large accountancy firms were more successful with their acquisitions than those that had either no advisers or advisers not in those groups.

Some CEOs insist on the involvement at such banks and firms of particular individuals they like or trust. For example, when Cadbury was being stalked by Kraft, it insisted on using certain senior managing directors and partners at the banks and law firms advising the company. Another example is Invensys, an engineering firm, which preferred to rely on the same adviser for each of its deals.

There are also market-leading "stars" at some investment banks with larger-than-life personalities. Such people are among a dying breed, but those still practising often make their way into the biggest deals, as was the case with the Kraft/Cadbury deal where, for example, the partner advising Cadbury in 2010 at Slaughter & May was selected to be the firm's overall managing partner six years later in early 2016. Another example from that deal was Bruce Wasserstein.

"Bid 'em up" Bruce

Bruce Wasserstein, CEO of Lazard, a financial advisory and asset management firm, epitomised flamboyant investment banking, using every lever – however aggressive – to secure a deal for his clients. There is no doubt that "bid 'em up" Bruce, as he was known to many in the industry, who died in 2009 while in the middle of advising Kraft on its takeover of Cadbury, was a Wall Street legend who shook up dealmaking in the 1980s.

Perhaps more than anyone, he symbolised private equity's determination to get its target, advising KKR on its ground-breaking take-private of food and tobacco company RJR Nabisco, an infamous deal that heralded the rise of financial sponsors and was described in a book, *Barbarians at the Gate*, by Brian Burrough and John Helyar, and later in a film of the same name starring James Garner as the CEO and president of RJR Nabisco.

Wasserstein's personal financial success in dealmaking also helped to seal his reputation – he sold his boutique advisory business Wasserstein Perella to Dresdner Bank at the height of the dotcom boom for nearly $600 million.

According to *Forbes* magazine, which put him on its cover,

Wasserstein "did more than anyone else to modernise investment banking by bringing aggressive tactics to a world previously known more for its clubbiness than its sharp elbows". He also fell out with lots of people, including his own partners. His public rows with Michel David-Weill, a descendant of the founders of Lazard – with whom he disagreed over his plans to take Lazard public – provided as much newspaper copy at the time as his takeovers.

Unsurprisingly, Wasserstein hated his "bid 'em up" soubriquet. Aside from the RJR Nabisco takeover – which was a financial success but loaded the target with debt – a few of the $250 billion of takeovers he advised on turned out to be disasters, including the Time Warner/ AOL deal discussed earlier in this book.

Wasserstein's death was much mourned. His former partner, Joseph Perella, called him "a rare talent". He certainly transformed Wall Street, pushing the envelope with creative legal interventions, direct approaches to shareholders and the active use of public relations.

Not everybody liked his style. With the global credit crunch came an expectation of corporate austerity together with disapproval from the press and public of sky-high investment banking salaries; a much quieter style of banker seems now to be in demand, certainly in Europe.

A football master class

Malcolm Glazer's acquisition of London Stock Exchange-listed Manchester United is a master class in how to pick off an unwilling target.

In 2003, Manchester United was one of the most successful football teams in Europe with a history that gave the club a uniquely popular global fan base. BSkyB, a satellite broadcasting company, had seen the potential for a combination two years earlier, but the regulators stamped on its bid as the fans launched a public campaign to stop Rupert Murdoch, the owner of BSkyB, from successfully buying the club.

It was a time when a number of outside investors saw the UK football market as an attractive investment for either prestige or money. In his book *The Glazer Gatekeeper*, Teshin Neyani says that others such as Russian oligarch Roman Abramovich (who purchased Chelsea Football Club) had already dismissed Manchester United as too difficult to buy and too costly. But Glazer, who already owned the Tampa Buccaneers, relied on his sports industry knowledge to identify extra value in Manchester United.

As in Vista's acquisition of Misys, the Glazers believed they knew the industry better than their rivals did. The family felt that the global marketing potential of Manchester United – and, more broadly, that of the UK's Premier League – was vastly undervalued.

Manchester United supporters publicly and vociferously hated the acquisition. In the run-up to the global financial crisis it became a cautionary tale against the use of debt in buy-outs: the Glazers paid £812 million ($1,471 billion), including transaction fees, to buy the club, yet put in just £240 million ($435 million) of their own cash. Whether by luck or good judgment, at the end of 2015 Manchester United was valued at almost £2 billion ($3 billion) and Glazer's children were taking £15 million ($22 million) a year in dividends from the investment. Not a bad return.

So how did they negotiate their way to such a great investment? Good industry knowledge and target selection took them part of the way, but their negotiating tactics made the difference. The family and their advisers knew that they were dealing with an unfriendly target that had no desire to be purchased. After all, why would the board of Manchester United want to facilitate the sale of a successful business, losing their own jobs in the process? Since the terms of Glazer's financing would not allow him to make a formal hostile bid for the company, he put the company into a bear hug.

In such a situation, sweeping up the market for available shares and building up a small initial (so-called toe-hold) shareholding are frequently used tactics, combined throughout with Glazer's effective use of UK company law. Glazer began to purchase shares in the company in March 2003 with small incremental stakes. Just six months later, in September 2003, when they hit a regulatory threshold, the Glazer family declared their holding to the public, as required.

By the end of the year, they had amassed over 14% of the shares from market sweeps and smaller shareholders, but only in February 2004 – when they were fully prepared – did Glazer announce that he was considering a bid for the company.

By November of that year the Glazer family had 28% of the shares and then demanded – and received – three board seats. At this point, however, Glazer was nowhere near being able to force through a deal. And the rest of Manchester United's board was still firmly against it.

But Glazer had a trump card in his negotiating strategy. The club's second-biggest shareholder with 29% was Cubic Expression, the investment vehicle of two Irish financiers and horseracing buffs, J. P. McManus and John Magnier. They also had a board seat. Combining his stake with Cubic's would give him more than 50% of the club – certainly enough for control and also sizeable enough to try to force out small investors.

As luck would have it, the two Irishmen had fallen out with Manchester United's long-standing manager and the company's most important member of staff, Sir Alex Ferguson. The Irish financiers had gifted Sir Alex part-ownership of Rock of Gibraltar, a champion racehorse, but when the football man also claimed the stud rights to the animal, a huge falling-out ensued, with Sir Alex suing and the Irishmen asking questions publicly about the financial probity of his transfer dealings for the club.

Between October 2004 and May 2005, the Glazers shifted into gear, making a series of incrementally rising indicative offers for Manchester United. But, in addition to receiving threats from fans (who themselves were trying to arrange a shareholding position to stop Glazer), they had still not secured the board recommendation they needed to take control.

In May 2005, they finally secured Cubic's stake, giving them a majority of the company's shares. Even then, while the Manchester United board advised shareholders to accept the offer on value grounds, it refused to recommend the bid, arguing that Glazer's highly leveraged takeover would be detrimental to the club's wider group of stakeholders including staff and fans.

Only at this point – though confident that they could squeeze out the remaining shareholders as would be possible under UK takeover regulations – did the Glazer family launch a formal bid for Manchester United. (The takeover timeline is shown in Figure 5.1.) Given the profit they have made from the club, the wait was worth it.

FIGURE 5.1 **Glazer's Manchester United takeover timeline**

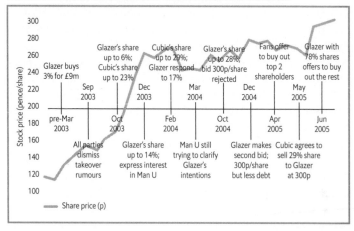

Source: Authors; public filings and press reports

Microsoft's search engine bid

If there is something the media enjoys more than a football takeover, it is a Silicon Valley merger. Like the Glazers' bid for Manchester United, Microsoft's 2008 offer for Yahoo! was played out in the full media spotlight. But although the Glazers clearly paid a top price for Manchester United, Microsoft's bid was about really big money in what the market calls a mega-deal: valued at up to $50 billion, it was merger games on a massive financial scale.

Just as the Glazers ultimately did, Microsoft opted to put Yahoo! into a bear hug. But in this instance – despite offering to pay 61% more than Yahoo's undisturbed market value – Microsoft failed to come away with the prize.

It is worth saying from the outset that Microsoft ultimately got lucky: Yahoo! signed a much less lucrative search and co-operation deal with it just one year later. Almost a decade later, its share price is still largely unchanged from the Microsoft bid price.

Microsoft has not had a happy time integrating some of the companies it has been able to buy. Yahoo! would probably have been particularly difficult in that regard and might have destroyed any value there was. For example, before it bought Skype in 2013, Microsoft's biggest deal was the acquisition of aQuantive, a digital-marketing services group, for $6.3 billion. It has since written off all but $100 million of the value of that purchase.

These failures reflect Microsoft's broader corporate and M&A strategy. In terms of negotiating tactics, it missed the opportunity to pull off what it had calculated was a deal worth paying for. Perhaps, like the Glazers with Manchester United, Microsoft saw something in Yahoo! that few others could.

Carl Icahn, an activist shareholder who tried to push the Microsoft deal through, was the forerunner of a host of activist investors at Yahoo!. Indeed, Yahoo! has continued to be the subject of takeover speculation as well as a target for other arbitrage hedge funds ever since.

Icahn's actions were central to the Microsoft deal and though not sufficient to push it through, are representative of the rise of activist investors. From the perspective of Yahoo!'s shareholders – who saw their company go through years of turmoil after the deal collapsed and who have seen its strategy drift ever since – the failure of the deal was a disaster. But assuming in terms of negotiation that the merger could have been good for both companies, let us consider what went wrong during that crucial negotiation phase.

Keep your friends close and your enemies closer

The technology industry may seem international, but it can be very local.

The Silicon Valley hub that produced Yahoo!, Microsoft, Google and Apple is a small, close-knit community – chief executives have often worked together, almost always know each other personally and certainly meet regularly at industry events. In early 2008, Microsoft's CEO, Steve Ballmer, was still working in the shadow of the company's larger-than-life founder, Bill Gates, who did not leave the firm as an employee until after the Yahoo! saga. Ballmer was facing a changed world dominated by Google, which was the runaway leader in internet-based computing. To tackle Google's dominance, he needed to make quick inroads into immediate revenue growth in paid-for search and display advertising. In the medium term, Microsoft also needed to protect itself against possible future threats from Google to its core Windows product.

Yahoo!, meanwhile, was on a downward trajectory, but was still a reasonably sought-after partner. A tie-up seemed like an obvious solution for both companies. Not only that, but Yahoo!'s shareholders – corralled by Icahn, who had a small stake in the search engine's business – were keen to arrest their company's slide.

Given the closeness of the industry, you would expect Ballmer to have known his target and its executive personalities well enough to pitch a good deal. If he was unsure, he might reasonably have been expected to put out some board-level feelers before making a public approach.

However, on February 1st 2008, Ballmer made an unsolicited $44.6 billion approach for Yahoo!. Press reports claimed background talks had been going on between the two sides for more than a year and – with the initial bid going in at a fairly full price – everyone expected the deal to happen. Instead, after ten days' deliberation, Yahoo!'s board rejected it.

Yahoo!'s response ten days later to that initial indicative offer was the standard one that it "substantially undervalued" the company, although it is notable that the market did not agree; the bid was well above Yahoo!'s share price and, when Microsoft walked away, the company's share price fell by a third. Media reports said this was simply an opening gambit and that Microsoft was prepared to bid as high as $50 billion. But Microsoft never did make a second, higher offer.

Yahoo! claimed as well that the bid was a "significant distraction", yet within a few days it began looking for a white knight by publicly cosying up to Microsoft's arch-rival, Google, as well as Rupert Murdoch's News Corporation. Trying to get rival bidders involved is a standard tactic for targets to get a higher price or to flush out more bidders, but in this case, in a bell-jar industry, it caused some seriously ruffled egos at Microsoft. Anyway, within a month, on March 11th, News Corporation walked away.

Had it been a bit more determined, Microsoft could have hunkered down and waited out the storm in pursuit of its long-term strategy. It certainly had the resources, including cash, to do so. Instead, despite the fact that analysts backed the tie-up, its quick departure looked distinctly like a childish sulk. This happened, according to the *Financial Times*, just days after Yahoo!'s founders, Jerry Yang and David Filo, supposedly flew to Seattle for a last-ditch negotiating session with Ballmer and Kevin Johnson, who oversaw Microsoft's internet operations.

The situation was complicated by a poison-pill provision in Yahoo!'s corporate regulations. In May 2001, the company had adopted a stockholder rights plan which stipulated that unless a deal was recommended by the board, shareholders would have the right to buy extra shares so that it could effectively block a hostile bid.

To be successful with a hostile bid, Microsoft would first have to persuade shareholders to get rid of Yahoo!'s board and replace it with pro-takeover executives, who would either rescind the poison pill or recommend the bid. Microsoft referred to this provision in its walkaway statement of May 5th 2008, when Ballmer said to investors in a letter that he had decided against this approach because it "would necessarily involve a protracted proxy contest" either for the shareholder vote or for changing the board.

However, Ballmer and his advisory team would have – or should have (see Chapter 3 on due diligence) – been well aware of this provision when they approached Yahoo! in the first place. This raises two questions: Why make a friendly bid unless you know it will be well received? And why make an unfriendly approach if you are not prepared either to go hostile or to play the long game and get investors onside? Regardless of history's judgment on Yahoo!, at the time Ballmer looked like a weak executive who had taken just one punch and then run away from a fight.

For Microsoft, that was the end of the Yahoo! merger saga, but it left the target in a difficult position. Several pension-fund shareholders launched lawsuits against Yahoo!'s management. Icahn, who continued to buy up shares, eventually helped to force out the CEO. Yahoo! ultimately signed up to a much less remunerative partnership deal on internet search and advertising with Microsoft over a year later in July 2009, leaving shareholders out of pocket and the company the proverbial tech industry "might-have-been".

Opening gambits: your place or mine?

First meetings between board-level executives of a bidder and target are often crucial to the success or failure of a deal, whether they are used to initiate takeover talks or to draw them to a conclusion.

Unfortunately for romantics, organised meetings between executives often take place in dull buildings. The days of high-powered chief-executive-level breakfasts or lunches in classic spots such as the River Room at the Savoy Hotel in London or the Rainbow Room at the top of New York's Rockefeller Center are, unfortunately, largely gone. Lawyers' offices are a particular favourite now: the uninviting grey exteriors of London's so-called magic circle of top law firms, or their equivalent in Frankfurt, Tokyo, New York and Shanghai, have provided cover for executives to meet and discuss the biggest deals of the past decade.

Quite why a tradition arose that legal advisers are considered to have more neutral venues than investment banking advisers – or accountancy firms – is unclear. Downtown meeting rooms in hotels are also commonly used: the anonymity of hotels is considered an advantage, as curious journalists may be less likely to note that two senior executives have met in a private conference room. Another well-used – and equally mundane – location for these jet-setting chief executives' meetings is a private corporate room at an international airport, such as New York's JFK or London's Heathrow, as often the CEOs are not based in the same city and someone needs to fly to the face-to-face meeting.

When it comes to floating the possibility of a merger with a rival – or discussing relations with a key investor – trade conferences can offer a more imaginative and informal opportunity. Indeed, the serendipity of meeting an executive at such a conference can lead to a discussion where the idea of an acquisition or merger is hatched, for later follow-up in the lawyer's or accountant's offices a few days or weeks after the conference. These trade forums may be even more important to buyers and sellers of small companies who may not be invited to global conferences such as Davos.

Trade relations

The World Economic Forum, held every January in Davos, Switzerland, is the king of international business conferences. Attended by politicians, bankers, financiers and the chief executives and chairmen of global corporations, this jamboree contains a higher density of billionaires and decision-makers than any other gathering on the planet.

Although a limited number of accredited journalists are invited, most attendees behave as if nobody is watching them. The public rooms provide a great opportunity for people-spotting; in 2010 for instance, any attendee could observe Irene Rosenfeld, then head of Kraft, deep in conversation with an activist investor, Chris Hohn. Rosenfeld had just completed the acquisition of Cadbury at a higher price than her key shareholder, Warren Buffett, would have liked, and observers were left wondering whether she might be expecting the rebel shareholder to register his concerns.

Further away from prying eyes at champagne-fuelled private parties sponsored by the likes of Google, Standard Chartered and McKinsey, a chief executive could float a merger in relative peace. The mountains behind the conference centre and those in Klosters, a nearby ski resort, contain dozens of upmarket chalets where private business functions can be held; the failed merger between News Corporation and UK-listed BSkyB was mooted in one.

Davos may be the king of conferences but it is actually as much a collection of politicians and country finance heads as of corporate senior executives. But there are other, more focused, industry events where deals can be casually raised. The annual tech industry conference run by Allen & Company, a US private investment firm, in Sun Valley has generated some important technology sector developments.

This conference, which has been going since 1983, offers whitewater rafting, tennis, hiking and yoga sessions. But, as at Davos, much of the work is done in private rooms or at the bar. For example:

- In 2008, key players in the Microsoft-Yahoo! merger, including Yahoo!'s president, Sue Decker, Google's founder, Sergey Brin, Yahoo!'s former CEO, Terry Semel, and some of Yahoo!'s major shareholders gathered for a chat.

- In 1996, it gained a reputation as a dealmaking centre when Disney's former chief executive, Michael Eisner, hatched a plan to buy the ABC television network.
- In 2014, it gave birth to the merger between AOL and Verizon. Although the deal was not announced until 2015, executives from both companies met a year earlier at the conference to explore possible commercial opportunities.

Fast or slow?

Some executives do not meet in a room together until a deal is about to collapse. In the case of Microsoft and Yahoo!, where there was interest on both sides in doing a merger, this was a terrible mistake and contributed to Microsoft's walking away. In other cases, it is a deliberate and successful strategy to keep the chief executives apart until the deal is almost done. Kraft made some bad mistakes in its 2010 takeover of Cadbury, but its decision to keep Cadbury's chief executive, Todd Stitzer, and chairman, Sir Roger Carr, at arm's length until the end of the deal was probably not one of them.

Kraft's chairman and CEO, Irene Rosenfeld, knew that she did not want to keep Cadbury's board or, particularly, the company's senior executives; she wanted the company's brands and its emerging-markets business. She also had challenges with her own share price as the offer was part-cash, part-shares and there were other issues simmering with the financing and investors. There was little need to speak to the target's board until she was in a position to make a proper offer.

The Baxalta bear hug

Early and focused engagement with the target's board and investors can be helpful in a bear hug, as illustrated by Shire's acquisition of Baxalta.

Companies that do their homework properly can complete the formalities behind a takeover quickly. Speed and surprise can also be advantageous tactics when mounting unsolicited takeover bids. One example is Shire's pursuit of Baxalta, a small US-listed pharmaceutical rival, in the second half of 2015. Shire, an Anglo-Irish company, surprised the markets by going public with an all-share $30 billion takeover offer for Baxalta in July 2015 at a premium of more than 35% to Baxalta's undisturbed share price.

The pursuit came less than a year after Shire was left at the altar by a larger rival, US-based AbbVie, as a result of US government opposition which derailed the agreed deal. One of the major attractions of Shire for US buyers was the potential to make tax savings thanks to the company's tax domicile in Ireland, where corporate tax rates are much lower than in the US. Once the AbbVie deal collapsed, Shire was free to pursue its chosen partner from the pool of pharmaceutical companies operating under the comparatively high US tax regime; as such, Shire had a lot to offer as a merger partner and acted quickly to take advantage of it.

Shire's pitch to Baxalta was that together they could become world leaders in the medical treatment of rare diseases, an increasingly lucrative field. The Anglo-Irish bidder not surprisingly – and with the backing of some analysts – argued that the acquisition would be to the benefit of both sets of shareholders, not least because of Shire's more advantageous tax regime.

Baxalta had been formally spun off by its parent company, Baxter Industries, for just one month when Shire announced its approach – the Anglo-Irish company reportedly informally approached its target just nine days after it had gained its separate corporate identity. Given the timing, it is likely that Shire – as with other good acquirers – had been monitoring its target for some time.

The offer was batted away by Baxalta's chief executive, Ludwig Hantson, who called it "puzzling". Shire's next move was to put Baxalta in a bear hug. Baxalta's corporate charter, like Yahoo!'s, included a poison-pill clause designed to fend off hostile takeovers. This clause stipulated that should a bidder begin trying to buy its shares on the open market, Baxalta could issue additional shares to incumbent investors once that bidder reached a stake of 10%.

The only way to get around the poison pill was to secure a board recommendation or to remove the board. In Baxalta's case the latter was made more difficult by a subsidiary defensive tool that meant board members' terms were staggered, so it would take longer to eject a majority of them as only a certain number could be replaced at any one time. Recognising the defences that Baxalta had in place, Shire focused its efforts on persuading shareholders to push for a board recommendation – something Microsoft could have done more effectively than it did in its bid for Yahoo!. Because Shire needed that recommendation, it structured the deal financially to appeal to Baxalta's board members, entitling them to multimillion-dollar pay-offs.

Shire's chief executive and chairman spent the next few months criss-crossing the Atlantic to press the case for the proposed deal with Baxalta's US-based investors. Their bold approach ultimately paid off when Baxalta's board accepted a sweetened part-share, part-cash offer valuing the company at $32 billion. Investors had made clear they wanted a cash element in return for their support, and Shire changed its bid to 40% cash, 60% shares. By this point, Baxalta's investors were pressing strongly for a recommendation and the target's board responded by agreeing to one.

Announcing the deal in 2016, Flemming Ornskov, Shire's chief executive, said revenue synergies from the merger could push combined revenues to $20 billion by 2020, compared with $12 billion in 2014. It is too early to assess Ornskov's promises, or whether Baxalta was the right target for Shire's shareholders. But what Shire did do was carefully select its preferred target and then make its move swiftly and with tenacity. In terms of negotiating tactics, this one was a blockbuster.

Still leaking?

Leaks, as discussed in Chapter 4, can be used by sellers as a negotiating tactic to increase leverage on buyers, for instance by forcing counter-bidders into the open. The myth of the accidental leak – the deal folder inadvertently left by an analyst in the back of the taxi – is just that, a myth. Most leaks look deliberate. And there are many, as Figure 5.2 shows.

Of the M&A advisers surveyed for the Intralinks study, half thought that leaks could be good for deals, although nine out of ten conceded that they could backfire. It is important to note that regulators take a dim view of firms and deals where there have been leaks, as they bring into question the integrity of the markets. The wrong kind of leak can get an adviser or a firm into trouble with the regulators.

Leaks are not restricted to the due diligence phase; they have much wider applications and deliberate leaks are used during negotiations.

FIGURE 5.2 **Percentage of deals which leak**

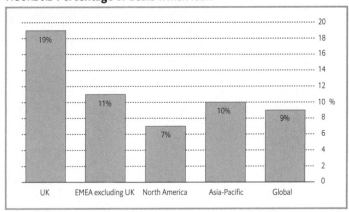

Source: *M&A Confidential*, IntraLinks, 2013

There is evidence that sellers use them to bring in rival bidders, and buyers use them to scupper a deal they are cooling on.

Although leaks are a tactic in the arsenal of unfriendly bidders, they are most damaging in a friendly context. Friendly deals are often announced with great fanfare, with deal completion plans, post-deal senior-management teams and even integration plans ready to be announced well advanced.

However, if a deal has to be prematurely announced because of a leak, these plans may not yet be fully developed, the pre-approval of key stakeholders and regulators may not have been gained, and the planning for the integration of the two companies post-closing may not have been completed. An early leak can mean the difference between success and failure, as Prudential's failed $30 billion bid for AIA, discussed in the next chapter, shows.

Negotiating tactics: dos and don'ts

- **Do** be aware that the first approach is usually the crucial one.
- **Don't** launch an approach until you are fairly sure how the target will react.

- **Do** your homework on any poison pill and other defences the target may have.

- **Don't** expect to be able to delegate the negotiations: the CEO and chairman will need to be involved in big deals.

- **Don't** be afraid to use a deliberate leak to move things along – but do be aware that such a tactic can backfire.

6

The engagement

COMMUNICATION – THE SECOND of the three big mistakes of dealmaking – is not just about the time when a deal is announced or, if you are unlucky, when it leaks. From the moment a CEO starts thinking about an acquisition strategy through the announcement of the deal to post-merger integration, a high-quality communications plan that takes in shareholders, employees and all the critical external stakeholders is not just a "nice to have" add-on. It is crucial for successful dealmaking and deal completion.

Listed companies nearly always have internal and external public relations advisers. But for smaller or private businesses, good communications need not necessarily involve hiring an expensive PR agency, as it can be done internally. The important thing is that somebody does it.

Most deals get done without the knowledge of a majority of the employees of both firms, with the obvious exception of start-up businesses, because the possibility that a deal might be on the cards could cause concern among employees as it often involves job losses. Even if this is not the case, deals are often a catalyst of organisational change and the notion of such a change on the horizon is likely to cause unwelcome distraction. The day of the announcement is therefore likely to be the first time employees of both firms find out that their work environment will change significantly. Most people do not like change, and surprises even less. So crafting a story about the reason for the deal, why it is a win–win situation and what it will mean for employees on both sides is paramount in order not to cause confusion, fear and ultimately the loss of key people. It is also a chance for the combined management to showcase a joint front line. This is especially important for the employees of the target company, who are likely to feel the least excited about having been taken over.

This chapter discusses the reasons for having a PR strategy and a plan to implement that PR strategy, whether or not you use an outside PR firm. It also looks at communications with shareholders – both institutional and activist – that are often handled by either management or their investment banking advisers. Finally, the example of Prudential's 2010 bid for AIA, the Asian arm of AIG, shows a communications disaster, where poor planning and communications scuppered what could have been a transformational merger for the venerable UK insurer.

Spinning tales

In the old days, PR advice on an M&A deal was an optional extra. Those days are long gone. In the past two decades, PR consultants – sometimes called corporate communications or financial communications consultants – are among the first on a CEO's speed-dial list.

Research by the Mergers and Acquisitions Research Centre at Cass Business School shows why there is a sound financial reason for this. *Selling the Story* reveals that it pays to pay for PR. The research, which examined 198 large public-to-public UK M&A deals from 1997 to 2010, found that deals with PR firms on board had a significantly higher chance of completion than those without. When PR firms advised both the bidder and the target, over 90% of the deals completed successfully, whereas those without any PR advisers did so just over two-thirds of the time (see Figure 6.1).

Given that PR advisory costs tend to be a tiny proportion of total deal-related expenses, hiring a professional communications team in a larger deal is both sensible and cost-effective. For smaller companies, it may even be a necessity, as they do not have other deals to fall back on.

In the words of Anthony Cardew of PR firm Cardew Group, whose clients include Smiths, Thorntons and Lonmin:

[PR advisers] play a very important role, especially in long-running M&A sagas, as long as they are sufficiently well connected to management to do their job properly; if a PR agency doesn't have the proper links with the management team it can't work in the same way.

FIGURE 6.1 **PR firms' effect on deal success**

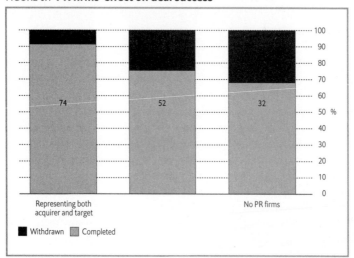

Source: *Selling the Story*, Cass Business School, 2014

It's certainly not just about talking to journalists on the day of a deal. You need to be spending time helping the company to communicate its long-term strategy to a range of stakeholders – whether you call that public relations or something else.

Another leading London-based PR expert, Chris Salt, a partner at Headland Consultancy, which advises clients including Danone, the AA, Legal & General and Johnson Matthey, added:

Many PR advisers will be in place long before a deal is on the horizon. Therefore, one of the key tasks would have been to work with the company to tell the corporate story in such a way that any bid or M&A activity makes sense in the wider context of a long-term strategy. And secondly, where some advisers might be just there for the deal, how one communicates during the deal process may have a strong bearing in the post-deal world for a company.

The timing of public-company deal announcements was also important. Deals announced before the start of trading were far more likely to be completed than those announced after the market opened. Deals announced between 7.15 am and 9.00 am had the highest completion rate at 87%; this fell to 64% after 9.00 am. Again, this points to good planning and a tight deal team with an ordered confidentiality process. Why? Because an announcement after the market is open is more likely to be one that is made in response to a leak or rumour, and therefore not one that was scheduled or planned in advance.

The content of the initial press release is critical, as it will set the tone for any subsequent media coverage. As in all things in life, first impressions are important, even to the hopefully dispassionate shareholders who will ultimately decide whether to approve the deal.

Even after the first public statements about the deal, the merging companies need to keep control – as best they can – of the external and internal communications. Sir Roger Carr, the chairman of Cadbury during its takeover by Kraft, described a meeting that took place each Friday to determine the PR strategy for the weekend in order to control the news reported in the Sunday press. The tone of those stories, he said, often determined how the press would react during the following week. This is especially important as there may be leaks (see Chapter 5).

Cardew talked about this:

Often reports of deals after leaks are only partially accurate, so if you are trying to justify an investment case it is really hard to row the story back to your territory because of the aggregate nature of the news media. There is a perceived wisdom it takes weeks to overturn ... Once a leak happens, you have to deal with the reality of it.

Salt added:

Leaks can be bloody annoying when you are on the receiving end. They often distort the position you and your client want to take and that can mean you lose time regaining the agenda. Having said that, there isn't a deal that exists where a strategy to counter a leak hasn't been considered and planned for. As to fatality? Rarely.

Of course, most companies will not be front-page news (as Cadbury was during the Kraft deal), and therefore most deals will not be subject to leaks. For these companies, control of the internal news grapevine is most critical. This internal communications strategy should be planned from the earliest stages of the deal. As Cardew says:

> A deal that is understood is going to be well received. What you've got to do is to tell a compelling story.

One element that appears in almost every deal announcement is a discussion of the potential synergies. This not only fully or partially justifies the premium that the buyer is paying, but also signals to the market what the buyer intends to do with the target. In Salt's words:

> Whatever may be your side's contention regarding anything involving a deal – not least synergies – you must be clear. Crystal clear. Or you risk losing your investment argument.

These synergy questions include:

- Will the target be fully integrated, leading to larger synergies? Or will it be kept principally as a separate division by the new owner?
- What will be the timeline for achieving those synergies, and thus will the changes to the two companies – but especially the target – be implemented quickly?
- How will the business model change?
- What will be the cost to achieve those synergies, and when?

Synergies are often an area where management, at least with the public figures provided, choose to underpromise and overdeliver. However, when there is resistance to the deal after announcement, it may be necessary to revise the synergy targets upwards and spending forecasts downwards.

Institutional investors: a CEO's best allies?

For publicly listed companies, institutional investors can make or break an M&A deal. Communications with institutional shareholders – and, where there is a large retail shareholder base, with retail shareholders – should begin if possible in the strategic phase. Any major move such as an acquisition or disposal should be signalled to investors well in advance and be part of both a coherent corporate strategy and a wider communications plan that also takes in the media and other stakeholders, particularly employees.

Early signalling – which is possible only when a company has its own strategy in good order – is crucial to the success of an M&A deal. Prudential's 2010 failed bid for AIA, the Asian arm of AIG, a US multinational insurance company, demonstrates what happens when a CEO suddenly and without warning takes his company in a very different strategic direction.

Listening to investors

Further research, *Learning from your Investors: Shareholder Support in M&A Transactions*, published in 2011 by Cass Business School's Research Centre, suggests that companies can learn and benefit from expert investors.

The study looks specifically at investors in a listed company that are likely to be either institutional investors (such as pension funds or insurance companies) that have particular geographical expertise, or sovereign wealth funds with good local access. These can all be harnessed by savvy management teams during the M&A deal process. The principle also applies to privately held companies where, for instance, private equity firms that own a stake in their portfolio companies will put one of their partners on the board of those companies, not just to keep an eye on the business, but also to offer fresh expertise and advice.

Companies that had such "monitoring" investors (those who manage their stakes actively) with superior regional expertise could expect to have more long-term success in cross-border M&A deals within that region.

Looking at a sample of investment into the UK, the study found that acquirers whose deals were supported by institutional investors with local knowledge in the target region clearly outperformed those without support. Acquirers with such support outperformed the market by 55.7 percentage points compared with those without it, which beat the index by only 6.3 percentage points.

One of the main aspects of the research is when the polar opposites of cross-border M&A strategies are compared:

- ■ "Blitzkrieg", where there is a rapid entry into a new foreign market through acquisitions, largely planned and conducted secretly.

■ "Playing the long game", where the company gradually works over time to build a dialogue between management and expert institutional investors in target foreign markets before entering.

The latter strategy may result in superior corporate performance and underscores the point that information should flow not just from management to the market but also in the opposite direction. The company needs a clear plan to get information from the market – here, for cross-border deals, according to the study, this should include those knowledge-intensive institutional investors.

Communication between management and public market participants such as institutional investors must be managed carefully, as any conversations may contain market-sensitive information. Exchange of sensitive and specific target information between the two sides could lead, in many countries, to the imposition of restrictions on an investor's ability to trade shares, as it exposes them to inside information not available to other investors.

Regulators will be on the lookout for any market manipulation or insider trading, so companies contemplating a takeover need to get in early. If institutional investors are fully briefed in the months and years leading up to a takeover bid on a company's overall strategy and general M&A plans (but not any specific deals or specific target companies), they will not need to have conversations later about market-sensitive information that would cause them to be "brought inside" with a consequent trading ban.

Rise of the activists

As well as introducing the public to the inside workings of a hostile takeover, the 1987 film *Wall Street* immortalised activist investing in the person of its anti-hero, Gordon Gekko. In the days when "greed was good" and "lunch was for wimps", Gekko and his ilk went by a less sanitised name: corporate raiders. These men (in those days there were no female corporate raiders) were stereotyped as the jackals of capitalism, hunting down and dismembering weak companies for profit without a care for the thousands of job losses that then ensued. Consequently, in the 1980s such men were also known as asset-strippers.

Since then the practice of activist investing has morphed into something perfectly respectable, a mainstay first of Wall Street and now of other financial capitals. Some of the original corporate raiders – most notably Nelson Peltz, through his hedge fund Trian, and Carl Icahn, now an active octogenarian – are still around. These days they are part of the establishment but nevertheless are still feared by corporate boards.

In the first decade of the new millennium they were joined by a host of arrivistes determined to shake up the companies in which they invest, using a range of tactics from the fairly hostile to the relatively friendly – all designed to persuade management to do what they feel is best.

According to a 2015 report by JPMorgan, a global financial services firm, entitled *The Activist Revolution*, funds under management by activist funds had ballooned from $12 billion in 2003 to $112 billion in 2015, with most of that increase taking place after 2009. In addition, multi-strategy funds (funds that use a number of investment methods in parallel) have refocused significant amounts on activist strategies. The report stated:

> *Adding to the dynamism of this asset class, new funds are entering the shareholder activism arena at a rapid pace (typically lieutenants of established or non-activist fund managers pursuing activism as a new strategy) and traditional institutional investors increasingly support – directly or indirectly – shareholder activist campaigns.*

Activists can tackle a range of issues from underperformance to poor governance, but often they seek to persuade management to drop a takeover that they feel undervalues the company to be acquired when the value of the company exceeds its current market capitalisation, or sell off non-core assets that the market undervalues. In some instances they may attempt to engage a board in private dialogue; in others they may go public with their case in the hope of mobilising a company's broader investment base. Or they start with the former but threaten the latter if the private dialogue does not lead where they want to go.

Activist investor Elliott Management, for example, applauded computer company Dell's 2015 acquisition of EMC, a data-storage systems provider, because it expected Dell then to sell off a number of divisions. Before the deal, Elliott had been pressuring EMC. Thus one company's acquisition became the foundation for potential future M&A deals through divestments, a topic covered in Chapter 9.

In the past, companies have batted activist investors away or attempted to ignore them, but today it is widely accepted that the best option is to engage with them as part of a broader cohesive PR strategy that includes investors, stakeholders and the media. Corporate advisers, principally investment banking and PR advisers, have a crucial role to play here. The JPMorgan report says:

> Today's activist campaigns are sophisticated public relations contests, fighting for the support of the company's shareholder base. Companies must approach their preparation and responses while keeping this new reality in mind.

Although it used to be common for boards to ignore activist shareholders that had a stake of less than 5%, smart boards have recognised that a strong activist's ability to galvanise the broader shareholder base means that they ignore such investors at their peril.

Indeed, companies are changing their corporate bylaws to allow these minority investors to exercise more control. In December 2015, Apple changed its bylaws to allow a group of up to 20 shareholders to nominate up to 20% of its board, joining other large US companies such as Microsoft, Coca-Cola and Philip Morris International that introduced similar changes in the same year.

Activism was born in the US, but activists are increasingly influential in Europe and Asia. JPMorgan reported in mid-2014 that 40% of activist hedge funds globally have either a European or a global investment focus. Despite their seedy reputation in their early days, shareholder activists have so far managed not to attract the attention of regulators. But this may be about to change.

Mary Jo White, chair of the US Securities and Exchange Commission, said that activists must be careful what they say when calling for corporate change. In early 2014 *Fortune* magazine reported her as saying:

*I do think it's time to step away from gamesmanship and
inflammatory rhetoric that can harm companies and shareholders
alike.*

Her comments came in the wake of stake-building by a US hedge-fund activist, Bill Ackman, in Valeant, a drug company, with which he was making a joint bid for its rival Allergen. Because Ackman knew about the bid ahead of time, a US judge examining the case said there were serious questions as to whether his fund had broken insider-trading rules. The very nature of what activists do in taking stakes in businesses and engaging management on strategy may make them vulnerable to market-manipulation investigations.

Yet at the moment they are riding high. Over the years, Microsoft, Cadbury, PepsiCo, Mondelez (formerly part of Kraft Foods), Time Warner, GDF Suez, Britvic, Lloyds Banking Group, Amec, Barclays Bank and even stock exchanges, such as the Deutsche Börse and the London Stock Exchange, have seen their takeovers – actual or planned – influenced by activist shareholders. No corporation is too big for them to target. They are here to stay.

Prudential's imprudence

In Europe the insurance sector emerged from the financial crisis in much better shape than the banks, having escaped its own liquidity crisis more than a decade previously. In February 2010, one of the most powerful and ambitious insurers was UK-listed Prudential, a global insurance company with booming emerging-markets interests.

Led by the charismatic Tidjane Thiam, Prudential was plotting a bold $35.5 billion (£24 billion) move to buy AIA, the Asian arm of cash-strapped US insurance company AIG, a business considered by many to be the jewel in its crown. The problem was not just that the markets were against Thiam, but that governments, regulators and investors were still reeling from the impact of the UK bank bail-outs and the euro zone looked to be on the brink of collapse. Thiam and his team also made a slew of mistakes in communicating the benefits of the deal to shareholders.

Robin Geffen, a fund manager at London-based Neptune who corralled the "No" campaign against the deal, later described it thus:

From the beginning it has been an absurdly ambitious attempt by the
Pru to buy a very large Asian company, at a very high price, with a
very unclear strategy.

Prudential's first communication mistake was that for its
shareholders, the deal came out of the blue; as Cardew put it, "anything
that surprises people is not good; the stockmarket does not like
surprises". Other shareholders must have agreed from the start, as
Prudential's share price dropped 8% within days of the announcement
due to concerns that included the amount of money that it would need
to pay for the deal.

Given that the acquisition would have doubled Prudential's market
capitalisation and dramatically shifted its centre of gravity from its
home markets in Europe to fast-growing Asia, management should
have known that the deal would be controversial. Although much of the
money raised by the £14.5 billion ($21 billion) rights issue was expected
to come from Asian sovereign wealth funds and the deal itself was in
Asia, management appeared to forget that it still needed the votes of its
long-standing UK institutional investor base to get it through.

According to the *Daily Telegraph:*

As one expert observer said: Tidjane wanted to fire his current
investors and get some new ones. He just forgot about the vote.

In this case the deal leaked before Prudential was ready to
announce, which goes some way to explaining the ensuing panic by the
insurer's board and advisers. But it is anyway generally safer to warm
up shareholders over a period of years if possible, not months, weeks
or days, when planning such a major initiative.

Thiam's troubles did not end there. He then faced a media storm
about his appointment to a seemingly innocuous non-executive
directorship at Société Générale, a French bank with its own significant
challenges. The media portrayed the appointment as a diversion and,
under pressure, Thiam turned it down.

But perhaps most seriously of all, as it was legally bound to do,
Prudential had failed to inform the UK's financial regulator at the time,
the Financial Services Authority (FSA), that it was planning to buy AIA.
This meant that not only did the insurer have to delay its rights-issue

prospectus, but also, in the regulator's eyes, the acquisition of AIA would leave it undercapitalised. Since this was a time when banks across Europe had collapsed and many were still considered as requiring possible government bail-outs, the FSA's ruling was extremely damaging. Although AIG was later able to negotiate a solution, the PR damage was already done.

Furthermore, in 2013 Prudential was fined £30 million ($45 million), one of the FSA's biggest-ever fines at that time, for failing to keep the regulator in the loop. Thiam was personally rebuked for his part in the failure. The FSA said:

> *The failure to inform the FSA was significant because it resulted in the FSA having to consider highly complex issues within a compressed timescale before making a decision as to whether to suspend Prudential's shares. It narrowed the FSA's options in scrutinising the transaction, risked delaying the publication of Prudential's subsequent rights issue prospectus and hampered the FSA's ability to assist overseas regulators with their enquiries in relation to the transaction.*

Thiam did manage to bring his core investors back onside. Three of the biggest – Legal & General, Janus Capital Management and Capital Group – backed his bid following a personal charm offensive by him and his chairman. However, Prudential was now presented with another problem: it had agreed on a final price with AIA, but in the wake of that agreement, financial markets around the world had tumbled further, particularly in the euro zone.

Prudential tried to renegotiate on price, but ultimately AIG – which by now was understandably concerned about Prudential's ability to get a deal done at all – turned the new offer down. Because Prudential's reputation had taken such a battering, it did not even try to revive its own deal. AIA was subsequently floated and its share price more than doubled in its first five years of being publicly owned.

So would Prudential's shareholders have been better off backing the deal? Thiam certainly thinks so. In 2014 he told investors that the company had missed a "once in a lifetime opportunity". He added, "I'm still animated about it. I apologise for not succeeding".

The Prudential deal is a great example of the "blitzkrieg" method compared with the safer and more gradual "playing the long game" strategy. Although there is a strong argument that the AIA acquisition would have delivered great returns, it is not clear that this was exposure that shareholders in Prudential, a conservative company founded in 1848, wanted. And for those that did, they could buy AIA shares when the company was floated anyway.

What do PR advisers suggest as best practice in this area? Cardew says:

> It's certainly not just about talking to journalists on the day of a deal. You need to be spending time helping the company to communicate its long-term strategy to a range of stakeholders – whether you call that public relations or something else.

He also suggests:

> A deal that is understood is going to be well received. What you've got to do is to tell a compelling story. It is absolutely crucial to lay down the context in which you might be announcing anything – what is your overarching narrative – a long time ahead.

In short, there are a number of pitfalls for dealmakers, and selling the story is one of the most important things to get right. This means that buyers and seller management need to address the question "What is our deal story?" early and devise a communication strategy as soon as possible in the deal process. For all kinds of stakeholders, both internal and external, good communication is crucial for large or small, public or private deals. Poor communication can scupper a public deal, as in the case of Prudential, but it can have even more devastating effects for a private transaction: the deal may go through, but because of poor communication the buyer loses most of the value as it fails to keep key people in the target and even in its own organisation.

The engagement: dos and don'ts

- **Do** treat your shareholders with respect – they have the power to derail the deal.
- **Don't** spring surprises on shareholders – they should be fully aware of your strategic objectives.

- **Do** make sure you have a communications team in place, whether internal or external.
- **Do** communicate, communicate, communicate and then when you finish communicating, communicate some more.
- **Don't** forget that the internal employees are just as important a target group for the communications strategy as the external press and shareholders.
- **Do** engage with activist investors – it will be easier in the long run.
- **Do** make sure all the details are in place before the announcement is made.
- **Don't** ignore regulators and other external stakeholders – you must have a communications plan in place for them, too.

7

Beware the regulator

A GROWING CONCERN for every ambitious company, particularly those targeting cross-border acquisitions, is the proliferation of regulators and governments that can and are willing to block the most coveted takeovers.

As the markets become ever more active globally, so too do merger-control regimes throughout the world, as countries bolster their national competition policies. This is true not just in the world's two major trading blocs, North America and the European Union; the Chinese government is also now much more active in its use of rules to regulate anti-competitive activity.

There are also increasing numbers of specialist national regulators that control mergers in particular industries, such as Ofcom, the media regulator in the UK, and the Food and Drug Administration (FDA), the pharmaceutical and health-care industries' regulator in the US.

In the US, merger control is policed by the Federal Trade Commission, the antitrust division of the Department of Justice and, ultimately, the Supreme Court. In the EU, the competition commissioner, a member of the European Commission, has responsibility for merger control. Possibly because its decision to block the transatlantic merger between General Electric and Honeywell put the European Commission on the global map in 2001, it is many of the EU's decisions that have been the most controversial.

The trend has continued in recent years. The regulator's move in early 2012 to stop a tie-up between two huge stock exchanges, NYSE Euronext and Deutsche Börse, even though the US had provided conditional approval just a month earlier, shows how crucial EU approval remains. Early assumptions that decisions were based on political connections were well wide of the mark, as the EU regulator continues to build its case law. Here, as shown in the other two case studies in this chapter, failings of communication and planning are most likely to create difficulties for bidders facing major regulatory inquiries.

Small private companies can fall foul of regulators just as easily as listed companies. The broad test is whether the newly combined businesses dominate their sector even within a narrow geographic area.

Another important issue for all bidders, but particularly those based in a different country from their target, is local rules specifically relating to "proper behaviour" during a takeover: the corporate law of takeovers, whether explicit legislation or legal case history. For example, under the UK's Takeover Code, which covers all transactions relating to publicly listed companies in the UK, all bidders for UK-listed companies are bound by the code, be they foreign or domestic. Sir Philip Green, a global retail and property magnate, famously fell foul of the code when he was held by the Takeover Panel to his promise that his doomed bid for Marks & Spencer was his final offer, since he stated publicly in July 2005 that "this is my final proposal", adding that if Marks & Spencer rejected it, "I'll go home". This statement prohibited him for a time from changing his proposal without the permission of the target.

However, such rules are easily overlooked by overseas bidders used to dealing with a different legal system. In this regard, Kraft in its 2010 bid for Cadbury may have overpaid because it did not take sufficient care to abide by these rules.

Another type of regulator is a country's national government. Governments around the world take their own approach to foreign investors. Most dramatic is the recent upswing in regulatory or legislative reviews through political intervention against foreign investments, with national governments considering the impact of takeovers on local jobs, economies and national security. Elected officials often use public statements to oppose or support M&A deals without having formal powers to do so, again as seen in Kraft's acquisition of Cadbury.

The "Danone law"

Government interventions in cross-border M&A deals can be hidden behind a veil of antitrust control or national security, as governments from France in Europe to the US in North America and China in Asia have done.

One example of a company protected by its government in obviously nationalist circumstances is Danone, a French dairy food group. Because of its narrow focus and relatively small size, Danone has long been viewed as an attractive target for large global food groups such as Nestlé and PepsiCo.

After the company's share price spiked in 2005 on a rumoured bid by PepsiCo, the French government stepped in with a law protecting certain industries from takeovers. The law was dubbed the "Danone Law" and was designed to protect strategic sectors, including those likely to have an impact on public order, national security and defence. It has often been joked that the company is strategically important for France because the army eats Danone yoghurt for breakfast.

The US government is not often viewed as one of the worst culprits in terms of protectionism, yet the Deutsche Börse case study later in this chapter shows that a government can step in even when there are no real national security issues. This case emphasises yet again the huge importance of good communication if you plan to launch a controversial bid.

Kraft's takeover of Cadbury hits a sour note

The £10.1 billion ($16.2 billion) takeover of Cadbury, a global confectionery company, by Kraft was a deal that had been years in the making. With key shareholders in common, particularly activist Nelson Peltz, a combination of the two companies seemed inevitable, even if it was unwelcome to the board of Cadbury, who hoped until the end to be saved by a white-knight bidder such as US chocolate manufacturer Hershey or Italian chocolatier Ferraro.

Having coveted Cadbury for years, Kraft was determined to get its target and looked likely to do so from the outset of its bid. There were no significant competition issues and the businesses were complementary, not competing, in terms of both products and geographies. Thus regulators were never in danger of derailing the deal completely. Yet Kraft certainly made mistakes that others can learn from – mistakes that fall absolutely within the big three.

Other than gaining the approval of Cadbury shareholders in the face of the opposition of the Cadbury board, the most high-profile hurdle for Kraft was the vocal opposition of UK politicians. The then business secretary, Peter Mandelson, warned that the UK government would scrutinise any foreign takeover of Cadbury and would oppose buyers that did not "respect" the confectioner. In reality, the UK government's actions were heavy on the bark and light on the bite. The UK is one of the most open countries in the world to foreign investors and is thus consistently one of the most attractive, according to Cass Business School's annual M&A market attractiveness survey. Its appeal is strengthened by its legal regime, as the UK cannot challenge foreign takeovers other than on grounds of national security.

Unlike the example of the French government and Danone, this definition is never really stretched and in this case the UK government made no regulatory challenge to the takeover. Here Kraft got it right; the company knew at the outset that its deal could not be blocked.

However, the deal did fall prey to errors in planning and communication, as Kraft ultimately needed the approval of shareholders, including some large UK institutional investors. To gain this approval, during the takeover Kraft promised keep open a factory in southern England. It made the promise in a bid to win over public opinion, but it did so without any real evidence of the factory's viability. Because it was a hostile bid, the bidder had no access to proprietary target-company information and certainly not the internal confidential plans to close a plant that would result in a large number of employee redundancies.

Once Kraft took over Cadbury, it found that the plant was not critical to the business and, indeed, that Cadbury itself had been planning to shut it down. Kraft therefore subsequently announced that it would be closed, leading to a massive public outcry. One of the consequences of this failure of planning and communication was that the company was twice summoned before an influential parliamentary committee to give an account of itself.

More critically, during the bid battle, Kraft breached the UK's Takeover Code. As Cadbury was in an offer period when Kraft's statements on factory closure were made, all company statements were being monitored closely by the UK's Takeover Panel. Under the code, companies in a formal bid situation are bound by any public statements about the takeover and must be especially careful not to say anything that is deemed to be untrue or misleading. The panel subsequently censured Kraft and its investment banking adviser Lazard for the mis-statements.

Such action by the panel is rare and thus was a significant embarrassment for both Kraft and Lazard. The fallout was most keenly experienced by Peter Kiernan, the Lazard banker leading the deal in the UK, who had recently been appointed as the next director general of the Takeover Panel and had to recuse himself after the ruling. With better planning and communication by Kraft and its advisers, this could have been avoided.

Kraft also fell foul of another important element of the Takeover Code which restricts a bidder's ability to change its offer. It made its initial bid partly in shares and partly in cash. Later, Kraft's CEO, Irene Rosenfeld, announced the company's intention to increase the cash component of its offer because some shareholders, most notably Warren Buffett, had complained that she was using too many of the company's undervalued shares to fund the deal. Under the provisions of Kraft's corporate constitution, by reversing the mixture from 60% shares/40% cash to 40% shares/60% cash, Rosenfeld was able to avoid putting the deal to a shareholder vote, thereby cutting out the disgruntled Buffett.

Rosenfeld may have had a good reason for doing this, but under the UK Takeover Code, once you are within a formal offer period, you cannot easily change the terms. To comply with UK rules, Kraft was not allowed to withdraw or amend its initial offer without the approval of the Takeover Panel and the target, which in a hostile bid situation was unlikely to be forthcoming. Effectively, Kraft would have to keep its old offer on the table in addition to any new offer, meaning it would be obliged to go ahead with the shareholder vote it was trying to avoid in the first place. This gave Cadbury a major tactical advantage.

As it happened, shareholder opinion was moving and investors wanted the higher cash component. Once Kraft signalled it would raise its bid to 830 pence per share from its original indicative offer of 745 pence, Cadbury's board agreed to open talks that ended with its recommending an offer of 840 pence per share, plus a 10 pence per share special dividend. Once it made that recommendation, Kraft would expect the Cadbury board to support its application to the panel to be allowed to vary its initial formal offer.

Kraft's initial failure, one of planning, is particularly instructive because this restriction on variation is a quirk of the UK regime; no such provision exists in the US. It is unclear whether Rosenfeld knew about the restriction when she made her initial offer, or whether she did but pushed on regardless. In this instance the mistake probably would not have stopped Kraft capturing its target, but because Kraft had to make a knockout offer to get a board recommendation, it probably did mean it paid more than it initially intended or hoped to pay.

The crucial lesson is that in cross-border acquisitions, all elements of the local laws governing the target must be explored and expert local advisers hired before any irreversible moves are made. This should be done as early as possible during the takeover planning. The importance of doing this can be seen by the high levels of outbound M&A since 2005, as shown in Figure 7.1, especially in some of the larger developed countries.

Deutsche Börse: you can't always rely on the Germans

The European Union was born of a Franco-German alliance that rose from the ashes of the second world war. Thus one perception in Europe is that if any company has the necessary political intelligence to negotiate a tricky European Commission antitrust inquiry, it must be a Franco-German one. So when the European Commission ultimately sounded the death knell of a merger between Deutsche Börse, Germany's principal stock exchange, and NYSE Euronext, a company itself formed from combining a major US stock exchange and a Paris-based stock exchange that encompasses Brussels and London, it came as a surprise.

It was a particular shock that the block came in the stock exchange sector, where exchanges are viewed as national infrastructure assets and arguments of national interest are particularly strong. Certainly

FIGURE 7.1 **Outbound M&A value per acquirer country** 2005–15

Country	Value ($bn)
United States	685.2
United Kingdom	435.4
France	305.7
Canada	237.7
Germany	234.9
Netherlands	226.1
Japan	197.5
Spain	170.4
Hong Kong	156.8
Switzerland	146.4
China	115.2
Italy	100.4
Belgium	91.7
Singapore	67.2
Russia	64.4

Deal value announced (excluding withdrawn) 2005–15, $bn

Sources: Cass research; Thomson Reuters data

Duncan Niederauer, the chief executive of NYSE Euronext, and Reto Francioni, his opposite number at Deutsche Börse, who had together lobbied hard and leveraged every personal connection they had to get the deal through, were taken aback by it. This was a friendly deal where both exchanges wanted to merge with each other.

In 2010 many of the world's stock exchanges rushed to consolidate. The London Stock Exchange and Toronto's TMX planned a merger that was on course for regulatory approval, although both companies later called it off for reasons unrelated to the regulators. Australia's ASX and the Singapore Exchange also tried to tie up, but they were stymied by Asian regulators. The merger between Deutsche Börse and NYSE Euronext was by far the biggest and boldest of the three deals and would have created a $9 billion transatlantic giant which would have dominated the global exchange market.

With a proposition of such dominance, you really have to sell the deal to the regulators. The two companies had a well-planned communications campaign, but they seem to have used the wrong forms of persuasion. They were playing a risky game by seemingly ignoring economic issues in favour of political ones and by concentrating on the wider European Commission, and in doing so going over the head of the competition commissioner, Joaquín Almunia, and his team.

The two sides presented the tie-up as an opportunity to create a Europe-based powerhouse able to take on the might of US exchanges such as NASDAQ and the Chicago Mercantile Exchange. However, they neglected the pure antitrust arguments within Almunia's purview. At the same time, as part of the commission's investigation, rival exchanges made convincing submissions to the competition commissioner that the deal be blocked, or only approved on the basis that the newly combined NYSE Euronext/Deutsche Börse would commit to make massive divestments in the areas where it would dominate.

By the time the European Commission came to a formal decision, the US antitrust authorities had already cleared the merger (albeit with some conditions), which was no small achievement for the companies and their legal teams. However, despite a year-long campaign by the two chief executives, the European Commission officially vetoed the deal in early February 2012, following a recommendation by Almunia. Despite the support that NYSE Euronext and Deutsche Börse had from a cabal of European commissioners led by Michel Barnier, a French commissioner overseeing financial regulation who backed the national champion argument, it was not enough. The commission, as it invariably does, ultimately supported the ruling of the competition commissioner.

Almunia told the *Financial Times* in an interview that the two companies had used the wrong approach:

> They tried a public relations campaign, lobbying, political pressure to get a positive decision. I told them from the beginning "you don't know how to deal with the commission". This is not the best way to convince us – quite the opposite, it is the wrong way.

In summing up why he opposed the merger, Almunia left little room for doubt: "The deal would have led to a near-monopoly in European financial derivatives worldwide."

Niederauer admitted that he had misjudged the competition commissioner's investigation into the market, which Almunia always insisted be considered on a pan-European not an international level. One senior person close to one of the two exchanges told the *Financial Times:*

> *Duncan has good relations with a lot of top European officials, including [International Monetary Fund managing director, Christine] Lagarde, and I think he thought he'd be able to persuade Almunia. But that was not going to work with Almunia.*

Angry at the outcome, Deutsche Börse threatened to take the European Commission to court to try to reverse its decision. Even after NYSE Euronext decided to walk away from the failed merger on the basis that a challenge would mean a protracted and expensive legal campaign, the German exchange insisted on pursuing its case, lodging it with the Luxembourg-based General Court of the European Union in 2012.

When it came up for review in March 2015, Deutsche Börse contended that the European Commission had not adequately considered that some merger efficiencies would have benefited customers, counteracting the negative impact of competition. It further argued that the commission had not properly taken consideration of the remedies it proposed, such as offers to sell off parts of the merged entity.

However, the General Court, the EU's second-highest authority, rejected the case, saying the commission had made no legal errors in its assessment of the market. As the European Commission is notoriously difficult to challenge and hardly any disappointed merger proponents ever try, few observers were surprised this time around.

There was a silver lining for Niederauer, a one-time executive at Goldman Sachs. NYSE Euronext was heavily dependent on him to provide it with a new direction once the merger fell apart, so it doubled his exit package to two times his salary as part of a pay hike. It also increased his potential equity bonus by $250,000. As for Deutsche Börse, it launched a bid in early 2015 for its London-based rival, the London Stock Exchange, in a deal structured as a friendly "merger of equals". For Deutsche Börse, it was a case of hoping that it would be third time lucky, as twice before, in May 2000 and December 2004, the London Stock Exchange had resisted merging with or being acquired by Deutsche Börse.

DP World: stuck in port

Even a relatively open economy like the US can sometimes resort to anti-foreign bias, as is demonstrated by the fate of the Dubai Ports World (DP World) bid for UK-listed P&O in 2006. P&O was at the time primarily a ports operator, having recently divested a number of businesses including its cruise-ship line, Princess Cruise. Its portfolio still included container terminals in a number of major US ports including Baltimore, Miami, New Orleans, New York and Philadelphia.

In a rapidly consolidating global marketplace for shipping infrastructure, P&O was a highly desirable target and a bidding war ensued between the Port Authority of Singapore (PAS) and DP World, a growing infrastructure business owned by the government of Dubai. On January 10th 2006, DP World made a bid for P&O, trumping the previous high bid from PAS, owned by the government of Singapore.

As the battle escalated, both sides moved to put in place the necessary regulatory permissions, the most important of which was an application to the Committee on Foreign Investment in the United States (CFIUS), a bipartisan political body that regulates overseas investment in the US.

At the time, CFIUS had the power to either approve a foreign buyer or open an investigation period to look into it more carefully; its powers have since been significantly bolstered. Historically, CFIUS tended to approve bids but there are some examples where it effectively blocked a deal by delaying it and causing attendant publicity. One example was a $18.5 billion bid by China National Offshore Oil Corporation for Unocal, a US oil company, which CFIUS blocked in 2005.

In January, a CFIUS panel chaired by the deputy treasury secretary and representing the views of the departments of state, justice, defence and homeland security voted unanimously to approve DP World's bid for P&O. Had any of the panellists objected, there would have been a mandatory 45-day investigation period and the matter would have been referred to the president for his personal clearance, but this did not happen.

Opposition to the deal grew as the M&A process moved on and P&O's board and shareholders approved a takeover by DP World. At this time, memories of the September 11th 2001 attacks were still painfully raw and the US still had more than 100,000 soldiers stationed in Iraq. Although Dubai, and the wider United Arab Emirates (UAE) of which it is a part, were key Middle Eastern allies in the so-called war on terror, Dubai also had some links to al-Qaeda: two of the 9/11 terrorists were from the UAE and some Dubai-based intermediaries had been involved in financing the plot.

The Bush administration tried persuasion to get the deal through, stressing the importance of the UAE to US interests in the Middle East and assuring the country that Gulf ownership of US infrastructure assets was perfectly safe. But critics of the deal, including Senator Hillary Clinton, drew no distinction between Dubai and other, less friendly, regimes in the region and continued to object. On February 22nd, the president threatened to veto any legislation Congress introduced to block the deal, but neither presidential persuasion nor force dampened the growing storm.

In this volatile environment some of the criticism of the deal was considered, linking security objections to allegations of cronyism by current and former members of the Bush administration, which had close business links to DP World. Other comments, such as on CBS's *60 Minutes*, one of the most-watched US TV news shows (see box), bordered on the racist and jingoistic.

Andy Rooney, CBS's *60 Minutes*, March 24th 2006

"A lot of Americans are concerned that it [the DP World takeover] might be a security risk. Security isn't what matters to me. What I don't understand is why the hell we can't run our ports ourselves. Too hard for us? Aren't we smart enough?

"Too much of our work is being outsourced. Why don't they outsource the White House? Or Congress? Get some really smart people from other countries to run ourselves for us. A Congressman gets about 162,000 [dollars] a year and all he can eat. I bet we can get some natives of Dubai to do the same work twice as well for half the price.

"I hope CBS doesn't decide to outsource *60 Minutes* and get someone from Dubai – Anwar Rooney – to do the work for a quarter of what they pay me."

On February 27th, in an attempt at damage limitation, DP World requested a 45-day CFIUS investigation. But by this point US politicians were asking for more. On March 7th, Jerry Lewis, Republican chairman of the House Appropriations Committee, said: "It is my intention to lay the foundation to block the deal." The next day his committee voted in favour of an amendment to do just that.

On March 9th, DP World capitulated, announcing a personal decision by the ruler of Dubai, Sheikh Mohammed bin Rashid al-Maktoum, to "transfer" P&O's US assets to a US-owned entity. Eventually the assets were sold to the asset management division of American International Group (AIG).

Reaction in the Arab world was furious. In a column in the Dubai-based *Gulf News* on March 17th 2006, political scientist Abdul Khaleq Abdullah said:

> *People, businesses as well as the government of the UAE are deeply offended as a result of the ports deal fiasco. People across the UAE are angry at the extent to which their moderate and open country has been demonised by the American media and lawmakers in Washington.*

The decision was a foreign-policy problem for the US administration and, in the longer term, a stain on the country's reputation as an open economy. It also had a big impact on US policy, leading to the Foreign Investment and National Security Act of 2007, which greatly increased the power and jurisdiction of CFIUS.

But is there anything DP World as a bidder could have done to avoid the fiasco? Possibly. There were clear errors in planning and communication, two of the three big mistakes of dealmaking. DP World made little attempt to "warm up" or lobby the broader body of US lawmakers or the public to the possibility of the ownership of US ports by a friendly Gulf nation.

A poll of Americans at the time revealed that they cared a lot about the nationality of port operators. Although, according to a Gallup poll, only 26% thought the federal government should not allow companies from the UK to own cargo operations at US ports, 50% would ban the French, 56% any Arab country and 65% China.

Any campaign to alter public opinion would have had to be long-running and persuasive to change such ingrained prejudices. But a well-planned PR and lobbying campaign that focused on the neutrality of DP World's arm's-length corporate ownership and reinforced the benefits of a merger might have had a chance of success.

What actually happened was that DP World, much like Deutsche Börse, thought it had regulatory clearance sewn up thanks to strong connections to the government, or in the case of Deutsche Börse the European Commission. DP World did not hire a lobbying firm until late on in the process when it sought to sway Congress to its side. But it was probably just too late.

Since the turn of the millennium, the likelihood of deals being blocked has increased significantly in EU and the US, and emerging markets are racing to keep up with Western regulators. In 2015 alone US competition regulators had a bumper year, blocking Comcast's $45 billion acquisition of rival Time Warner Cable, Tokyo Electron's $30 billion takeover of US chipmaker Applied Materials, and Electrolux of Sweden's $3.3 billion bid for General Electric's vacuum business. Regulation is here to stay.

Beware the regulator: dos and don'ts

- **Do** remember that even if shareholders agree to a deal, the government can stop it.
- **Do** know who in the government is making the final decision, whether regulators or politicians.
- **Don't** assume that takeover rules are the same in another jurisdiction.
- **Do** abide by the rules.
- **Don't** forget that communication with regulators – and with influential politicians and the public – is crucial.

PART 3

Post-deal

8

Doing the deal right

FRANKLIN D. ROOSEVELT took office as president of the US in the depths of the Great Depression. The country had been ravaged by several years of runaway employment, deflation and falling output, and Roosevelt knew he needed to act quickly. Between March and June 1933 he introduced numerous measures to prime the pump of the US economy, including the Glass–Steagall Act, which safeguarded the financial infrastructure of the country through the legal separation of commercial and investment banking until it was repealed in 1999.

Roosevelt's so-called New Deal may be a little too Keynesian for the tastes of some in business today, but the method by which the policy was implemented was the political forerunner of a major corporate concept: the first 100 days. The 100-day turnaround timeline – which can be traced back to Napoleon Bonaparte, who returned from exile, reinstated himself as the ruler of France and declared war on the UK and Prussia before capitulating at the battle of Waterloo just over 100 days later – is used in business by incoming executives and owners to provide a structured action plan that puts a company on the front foot. It is a fundamental part of M&A strategy.

A successful M&A strategy – and the beneficial impact on the wider economy discussed in the Preface – starts with doing the right deal, at the right time. This principle is the subject of the first seven chapters of this book. The second part of the equation for success, and the subject of this chapter, is doing the deal right. The latter typically attracts less attention and scrutiny than the former, but it is, in our experience, where real value can be added or destroyed, irrespective of the rationale for the deal.

The 100-day plan is corporate shorthand for deal integration and a key part of it, but it is by no means the whole. Deal implementation begins with the disciplines discussed in Chapters 1 and 2, where you formulate a deal strategy in line with your company's overall strategic aims and rigorously target acquisitions that can deliver this. Determining whether you have the capacity to spend the time and resources on integration should be part of the planning discussed in Chapter 1. More specific post-closing planning for the integration should begin as soon as a target is identified and should be an intrinsic part of drawing up a list of target companies (see Chapter 2). After all, how can a deal be costed and its benefits and synergies assessed until you have at least a skeleton integration plan? This chapter should be read in conjunction with Chapter 3 on due diligence, which, if done properly, will provide the foundation for the integration of your new business, highlighting any particular issues that may arise in terms of culture, people, processes and indeed almost every aspect of the newly combined business.

Of course, the other chapters are also critical to this integration: Chapter 4 – can we afford the costs of integration and are these built into our value model?; Chapter 5 – have we negotiated properly to keep the people and resources necessary to do the integration?; Chapter 6 – do we have a plan for communicating all of this to our various stakeholders?'; and Chapter 7 – have we anticipated the regulatory responses in terms of the impact on deal closing?

Clearly, a deal's longer-term success depends on what is done on integration throughout the deal process, including the post-announcement and post-completion periods. Particularly important is capturing planned synergies and raising staff morale as quickly as possible to realise the deal's potential. In times of economic uncertainty and low growth, delivering the full and promised value of acquisitions becomes even more important. The success of a transaction is often defined by the ability to deliver the promised synergies, of either revenue or cost, and to implement a change in operating model. This is crucial, and applicable to all sizes and types of deals, public or private, including deals among charities.

An excellent example of the latter is the Royal National Institute of Blind People (RNIB). On April 1st 2009, the RNIB formally announced that Action for Blind People (Action) had become the third member of its sight-loss group alongside National Talking Newspapers and Magazines and Cardiff Vales and Valleys, the first three of many more in the RNIB's consolidation of related charities in the UK. The formation of this group cemented the RNIB's position as the leading sight-loss charity in the UK.

The driving force behind the mergers was both financial and political, but the vision came from the RNIB's CEO, Lesley-Anne Alexander, who felt that having over 700 charities in the UK seeking to achieve the same objective was counter-productive to achieving their charitable objective of providing the best possible support for blind and partially sighted people.

The RNIB recognised that there could be significant synergies in these mergers, as, for example with this deal, the services provided by Action, which were primarily community-based and in England, would complement its own services, which were based specifically in Scotland, Northern Ireland or Wales when not national. The combination would therefore fully cover all the regions of the UK for all its overlapping services, thus enabling it to gain the maximum return from its increasingly difficult quest to raise funds.

So a decision was made to combine operations and a five-year partnership deal was entered into. It involved Action taking responsibility for all the RNIB's and Action's regional and contract services and staff in England, and the RNIB taking over fundraising for both charities. The deal reflected the fact that front-office operations were to merge but back offices were to stay separate.

Alexander commented on the realistic achievement of the synergies and benefits of the merger:

Before we did anything with Action we had 0% of the benefits of the merger, and possibly if we had done a traditional takeover and merged completely the front office and back office, we would have got 100% benefit. I estimate that with the new structure we achieved about 50% of the benefit. In my book, 50% is a whole lot better than 0% and the door is open to increase from 50% as time passes.

That benefit is derived from blind and partially sighted people having one place to go for their services, on the high street in Liverpool, Birmingham, Bristol and Manchester, and all those other places where we have a presence. Everyone says economies of scale can be derived from merging back office activities but that was not on offer and I was not going to be prevented from merging front office – the real places that real blind and partially sighted people visited – because I could not have it all! I can put up with back office complexity if that is the price we are paying for making the landscape simpler for our service users.

Crucially, the pre-completion integration phase also operates as a canary in a coal mine for a deal. If the headline integration plans – such as the selection of an executive board – are coming unstuck, this is a definite signal to walk away. Similarly, if the market shifts during the negotiation phase, this might be a last opportunity to get out and avoid the sort of corporate Armageddon experienced at RBS.

Integration can mean a complete blending of the two businesses from the executive level downwards, or completely separate businesses (common with private equity portfolios), or anything in between. What matters is that the post-closing phase is properly planned and that the rationale for buying the business is implemented in expertly rendered fine detail.

Broadly, the integration process can be broken down as follows:

- Phase 1: Pre-closing
  - Stage 1: High-level merger planning. Discussion restricted to a small group of senior executives representing the key areas of integration, avoiding leaks.
  - Stage 2: Announcement. The expectations of management and employees should be carefully managed from the outset. At least the top level of management, if not the second, should be in place by this time.
  - Stage 3: Informal integration. The more uncertainty, the more unstable the target organisation will be. It may be essential at this point to begin the combination of particularly challenging systems, such as IT and HR systems, if possible, or at least to be planning for this. If the negotiations turn sour at this point, be prepared to walk away.

- Phase 2: Post-closing
  - Stage 4: The 100 days, the key window to set up the right foundations for integration.
  - Stage 5: Stabilisation and organisational and cultural integration. This is a long-term process and can take several years to finalise. The journey is complete when employees, customers, suppliers and investors consider the combined company to be "business as usual" and when few refer back to the legacy organisations. A good rule of thumb is that this stage should not last more than three years, and ideally be much shorter.

As a deal moves towards completion, the corporate team steering group is likely to change, with new personnel – either in-house or external advisers – taking over from the deal-negotiation team. However, it is important that communication and handover between the teams are good, with at least some executives providing continuity or working alongside each other for a specific time period. Disconnects between the two teams can be and often are among the biggest impediments to the proper implementation of the developed integration strategy.

In addition, throughout the process, management needs to remember that the biggest challenge may not be the integration but making sure that employees keep the core businesses running successfully.

Phase 1: Giving diligence its due

Good integration begins with good due diligence, which means using an issue-led approach to identify and address the key issues at the outset, instead of falling back on a compartmentalised, box-ticking approach of separate tax, financial, legal and other assessments. Time and time again companies pay for due diligence (advice), then throw it away once it has been used to establish a price.

Comprehensive due diligence information should be used to provide a blueprint for the post-deal integration that will allow a buyer to maximise its financial and strategic goals and avoid the pitfalls that have been identified. In this way good due diligence should easily pay for itself. This blueprint of the merged business should set out the principal elements of its new strategy, reiterating the value drivers for the deal outlined when the target was first selected.

There should be a clear idea early in the deal process of what the merged company will do differently compared with the target's – and perhaps even the buyer's – former business plans. Once this is identified, the CEO – yes, the process needs to be led throughout from this level – should comprehensively allocate responsibilities to selected senior managers so that it is clear to all who has the responsibility to implement the plan. This needs specific timeframes and milestones and should be clearly linked to management performance targets and assessments.

Once that is done, management should develop a clear day-one plan that specifies how the new combined organisation will operate from the outset. Despite the point made earlier about a damaging disconnect between the deal-negotiation and implementation teams, it can – provided there is sufficient oversight – be advantageous to use a so-called "clean team", comprising internal staff and external advisers, to prepare this plan. Such a team will operate between both organisations and develop integration plans and business cases consisting of commercially sensitive information that normally could not be shared between the announcement and completion phases of the deal. This is particularly important when there is a hiatus between the recommendation of the deal to stakeholders and the date of closing, for instance where there is a lengthy regulatory review.

The day-one plan should also be designed with maximum flexibility, as better information will be available in phase 2 (see below); the integration plan should allow for changes using that new data. This is also the point, if the deal is not going to plan, at which to consider whether to press ahead or cut your losses and step aside.

Off the rails: stopping runaway trains

By the time a deal is nearing completion, a buyer's management team will have invested months, or possibly years, of executive time in planning the takeover. They will have paid advisers and may have arranged deal financing. In such a situation the momentum behind an acquisition will be such that the team will feel the only possible way is forward.

The best chief executives have not just the ability to spot a losing hand, but also the courage to fold when necessary, even if they have taken a big financial gamble on an acquisition. The Omnicom/Publicis merger outlined below descended into ever more public rows about board representation until it was called off in 2014, clearly picking up on a classic sign that a deal had not been properly thought through. Trains tend not to fall off the tracks with no warning. Here, as is often the case, failures in strategy – and most importantly in due diligence – are what unbalanced the carriages.

Holding hands across the Atlantic

When France-based Publicis and US-based Omnicom announced their $35.1 billion merger in mid-2103, they raised the tantalising prospect of a PR and advertising giant that would combine the accounts of global super-brands such as Pepsi and Coca-Cola and provide real competition for the sector's biggest player, WPP.

According to the *Financial Times*, this rare "merger of equals" began with a joke. Omnicom's chief executive, John Wren, was visiting Publicis's Paris headquarters in 2013 when he paused to admire the outstanding view from the rooftop, which overlooked the Arc de Triomphe. Maurice Lévy, Publicis's chief executive and Wren's long-time rival, replied, "It can be yours" – and thus the idea of the deal was born.

The combination of the two listed businesses seemingly made perfect commercial sense. In an era where massive new internet and social-media players, such as Google and Facebook, typically wanted to work with agencies close to their own size, smaller-scale companies felt that business was passing them by. A merged Omnicom/Publicis would have been much larger than WPP, with US revenue alone of $11.4 billion (twice as much as that of WPP), and would have been in pole position to deal with the new media and technology giants. Even the timing of the merger was perfect; in 2013, advertising was finally emerging from the slump it fell into during the financial crisis and subsequent recession.

Yet by the time the deal was announced in July, talks aimed at creating a management structure for the new business were already stalling. The two companies are "people businesses" whose job it is to be emotionally intelligent and sensitive to clients' needs. It is probable, however, that in their own deal they forgot when doing proper due diligence that consideration of these human factors is crucial. As discussed in Chapter 3, corporate culture and ways of working or operating are often overlooked during the due diligence process, but it is on this rock that takeovers can crash. It is vital that executives consider the soft cultural issues, as they are often outward manifestations of very different management styles and ways of working, and an indication of how far power is devolved within an organisation.

Within the advertising sector, Omnicom and Publicis – and their two chief executives – could not have had more different corporate cultures. Wren, an American, was a former accountant who kept a low profile in a glamorous industry, whereas Lévy, according to the *Financial Times*, was a European charmer with a real year-round St Tropez tan. These different styles, probably reflected deeply in the two organisations, are issues that should have been identified early on in the due diligence phase and an action plan drawn up to deal with them.

What actually happened was that the two men agreed on the most important jobs in the business – their own – as a precondition to a merger. They would share the job of chief executive for the first 30 months, then Lévy would step up to the role of chairman. However, they did not go much further. In most mergers, it is important to identify most or all of the senior executives at the outset. This is particularly true if the deal involves people businesses, where human resources are the companies' biggest asset or where management has specialist expertise that is crucial to the success of a merged business (witness the example in earlier chapters of HP's purchase of Autonomy). And it is doubly true where the two businesses are similar in size and power and therefore the merger of equals idea is real, or close to it. A similar issue arose in Chapter 3, when Britvic and A. G. Barr decided not to restart their merger talks in part because they could not agree on board roles.

The flashpoint came for Wren and Lévy over who got the role of chief financial officer. Both men wanted to make this crucial appointment and realised it was key to getting their vision imposed on the overall business. Because the culture of the two businesses was different

– Publicis was highly centralised and Omnicom highly devolved – this was a particularly important appointment. Claudio Aspesi, an analyst at Sanford C. Bernstein, said:

> It was only human for both CEOs to want their trusted staff around them but you can only have one CFO.

But according to Lévy, Wren also wanted to bring across his general counsel, meaning the two most important financial and legal functions of the Franco-American business would be filled by Americans, an outcome that was culturally sensitive for Publicis. Lévy told the *Financial Times*:

> The balance was not being respected. He wanted to have his CFO as CFO, and his general counsel as general counsel. So as you can see, the key positions of the holding company would have been in the hands of Omnicom people and this was unacceptable.

A number of tax and regulatory issues also raised their heads and, in 2014, the two sides called the deal off.

In a joint statement the two CEOs said:

> The challenges that still remained to be overcome, in addition to the slow pace of progress, created a level of uncertainty detrimental to the interests of both groups and their employees, clients and shareholders. We have thus jointly decided to proceed along our independent paths. We, of course, remain competitors, but maintain a great respect for one another.

Lévy said separately that Publicis's founder, Marcel Bleustein-Blanchet, would have "turned in his grave" over the proposed merger and that his company would stay single.

Other obstacles on the tracks

Some deal processes should just never have been started. But what should you do when the market shifts around you in a way that you had not – but should have – anticipated, or perhaps could not even have foreseen, the proverbial "black swan" event? In the standout example of the former, in the banking sector, RBS pressed on with its ill-conceived pursuit of ABN AMRO as the financial storm clouds gathered in 2007 after its rival, Barclays, gave up on the deal.

With oil prices falling thanks to falling demand and the impact of new North American sources on supply, how will consolidation in the energy sector be affected over the next decade, and have deals already in the pipeline been affected?

Many deals have rightly been called off because the markets, including the competitive environment, have changed since the deal was first conceived. If, for example, RBS's chief executive and board had been less driven by ego and more by the markets, the bank could have avoided the disastrous takeover of ABN AMRO (see Chapter 2).

As discussed in Chapter 4, the merger mania that hit aluminium and iron-ore producers, including Rio Tinto and Glencore Xstrata, did not look as well conceived following the collapse of commodities prices; the commodities super-cycle theory beloved by Rio Tinto's Tom Albanese and others turned out to be subject to exactly the same cycle of boom and bust that has always governed the economy. BHP Billiton had what may have been a lucky escape from some of the fallout from the collapse of commodities prices because it abandoned its 18-month pursuit of Rio Tinto in 2008 just as the downturn began.

The decision to drop Rio Tinto was due in part to the hostility of Chinese regulators to the deal, in part to shareholder opposition to it, and in part to turbulent markets that made it difficult for BHP to secure the financing for the takeover. In this case, it listened to outside signals.

When BHP walked away, however, it blamed the collapse of its transformational merger on the end of the super-cycle. BHP's CEO, Marius Kloppers, is quoted in the *Wall Street Journal* as saying:

> This decision is set against the global economic crisis and its impact
> on our assessment of its benefits ... I think the commodity prices across
> our suite of assets and for most of the other players have gone down
> by 50% over the last six weeks. It has clearly impacted our cash flows
> already.

Hitting the political sidings

The world's regulators and politicians have a large and growing influence over the fate of the biggest and most important deals. In many cases there is simply no getting around the regulator, especially (as seen with Danone in Chapter 7) if the politicians in question are French and believe their country's army marches on its yoghurt. This sort of overwhelming opposition to a takeover simply cannot be fought, or a least not without a campaign over decades or some hefty political influence.

Many companies will wish to "kick the tyres" to establish how far they can push expansion and will do so in the full knowledge that they will have to spend money on advisory fees and time on an exploratory deal to get a firm answer to their questions. The difference between those that have a good M&A strategy and those that do not is that the former know when to walk away.

In 2012, two of the world's largest defence and aerospace companies, UK-based BAE Systems and France-based EADS, had a tilt at a merger that would have catapulted them into the same league as US companies like Boeing and Lockheed Martin. The tie-up faced huge political and regulatory hurdles from the outset; the UK, France and Germany all had stakes in the businesses and even the US, BAE's biggest client, took an interest in its ownership. A month later the two companies called the deal off saying:

> It has become clear that the interests of the parties' government stakeholders cannot be adequately reconciled with each other or with the objectives that BAE Systems and EADS established for the merger.

The two sides had managed to agree on strategy, management and even dividends. They had initial support from the UK government, which had a "golden share" in BAE that allowed it to block a deal if it wished, and traction from the French government, which owned 15% of EADS. But they had failed to convince Germany, which held a stake in EADS through carmaker Daimler.

On one interpretation, the deal's collapse was a failure, and could have left BAE vulnerable to unsolicited takeover bids. However, on another, the companies managed to close down one avenue quickly

FIGURE 8.1 **What strategies are available?**

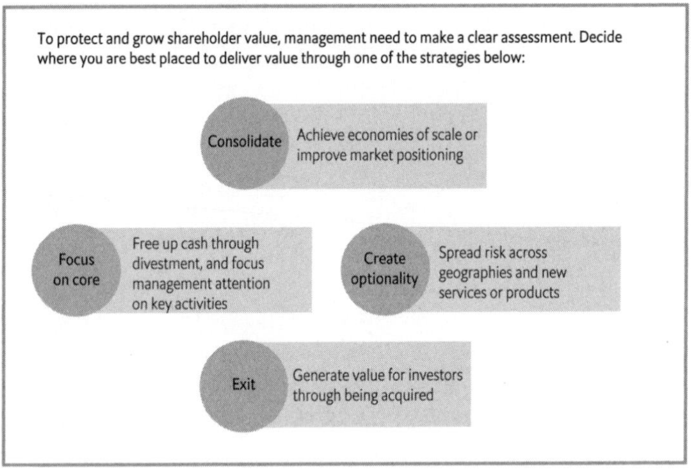

To protect and grow shareholder value, management need to make a clear assessment. Decide where you are best placed to deliver value through one of the strategies below:

Consolidate Achieve economies of scale or improve market positioning

Focus on core Free up cash through divestment, and focus management attention on key activities

Create optionality Spread risk across geographies and new services or products

Exit Generate value for investors through being acquired

Source: *Oil Pressure*, EY, 2015

with little loss of management time or damage to their reputation. Contrast this with Deutsche Börse, which fought to the end – and beyond – in an attempt to force regulators to back its merger with the NYSE. Where there is real regulatory risk, knowing when to cut your losses is crucial.

However, dramatic market movement alone should not necessarily mean that a deal should be abandoned. Falling prices can be a driver of industry consolidation, which is one of the four strategic options available, as shown in Figure 8.1. Oil prices fell by around 50% from the middle of 2014 to the end of 2015, but against this backdrop the oil and gas industry has seen a wave of consolidation. The trend echoes what happened when oil prices were similarly depressed in the late 1990s, a period when BP joined forces with Amoco and Arco, Chevron combined with Texaco and Exxon with Mobil. According to the *Financial Times*, private equity firms including Carlyle and Blackstone have in parallel raised billions of dollars to spend on oil and gas acquisitions in the expectation of companies' disposing of non-core assets.

The guiding principle when making tough decisions should be to look back at the original deal rationale and due diligence. Will a merger still deliver the strategic wins identified? If the answer is yes, pushing ahead may be the right thing to do. If not, you should have the courage to walk away. Again, this is no different for a small or medium-sized company that is undertaking a deal. Reassessing and walking away is just as important for smaller companies or private equity firms, such as Gores Group, which in 2012 walked away from a deal with auto and parts repair company Pep Boys. In that deal, despite nearly two years of discussions, the buyer decided that poor financial results in the target meant that the deal could not proceed.

Phase 2: Day 1 of the 100-day plan

In a takeover situation the buyer will never have access to all the information it would like. This is particularly true in a public deal or a hostile deal where access to proprietary internal due diligence is limited or even non-existent.

Following completion, however, as the proud new owner of the target, the acquirer can recalibrate its original deal rationale against a new set of data. From then on, it can review integration plans against the real numbers and facts while the 100-day integration plan is being implemented. Reviews should be regular and often, allowing management to monitor progress against the original aims of the deal.

In most deals, the delivery of synergies – defined as the financial benefits of cost savings and revenue growth attributable solely to the combination of two previously separate companies – will determine the success or failure of the enterprise. Many buyers will already have outlined a timetable for the achievement of synergies in pre-closing conversations. For public companies in the UK and some other jurisdictions, this description and quantification of savings is required in the formal merger documents filed with the regulators.

One technique for determining synergies is triangulation, a process that evaluates identified synergies (cost and revenue) and compares them with the historical delivery track record and external industry-specific benchmarks. By comparing the identified synergies in this way, buyers gain a substantial indication of the robustness and size of the identified synergies.

Our experience suggests that stakeholders, such as financial institutions, have three main questions:

- How much are the synergy benefits worth? Are they cost- or revenue-based, or both?
- When will the synergies be delivered? Transformational change should be done at a reasonable pace to extract the maximum overall benefit.
- To achieve those synergies, what one-off costs are estimated in the integration programme? Has management completed a robust analysis of these one-off costs required to deliver the identified synergies (cost and revenue)?

Once this has been established, synergies should be made a priority part of the integration plan, with internal targets often 20–30% higher than those made public – the "underpromise, overdeliver" point discussed as a PR tactic in Chapter 6. In addition, the costs to achieve those synergies, which often cause pain in the organisation due to employee redundancies and the closure of plants or business lines, should be taken early. Delaying the inevitable does not make it easier and may indeed make it more expensive.

Of the factors that determine whether M&A adds or destroys value, integration is arguably the most important, although it is possible for an acquisition to be a huge financial success even if it is never integrated into the parent company. What is important is that the rationale for the deal is sufficiently well enunciated ahead of the deal in order to determine properly what the post-deal operating business model of the combined organisation will be.

Unsurprisingly, it is clear that serial acquirers are better at integration as well as at target selection (see Figure 8.2). In a report published in 2016, management consultants A. T. Kearney found that the enterprise value growth rate of serial acquirers (those doing more than five deals per year) was 25% higher than the growth rate of companies that made no acquisitions. The examples given in Chapters 2 and 3 certainly fall into this category – from Diageo's emerging-markets targeting triumphs to CKI's due diligence machine. Time and again, buyers that get the fundamentals right have the tools they need to continue building post-deal integration and beyond.

FIGURE 8.2 **Serial acquirers create value faster than other companies**

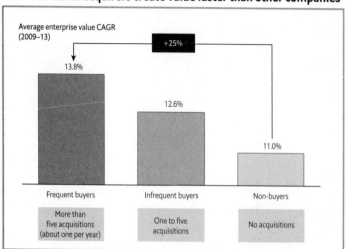

Source: *M&A Muscle*, A. T. Kearney, 2016

Getting it right: the Centrica way

When Venture Production, an oil and gas exploration and production company, grudgingly accepted defeat in 2009 in its battle to thwart a £1.3 billion ($2.2 billion) takeover by Centrica, the UK's biggest utility company, the history of the tussle did not bode well for a successful integration.

Centrica had acquired its new division by way of a hostile takeover bid in which it appealed to Venture's shareholders in the teeth of strong opposition from the company's management. Even when Centrica captured 50% of the company's shares and its board finally recommended that investors accept Centrica's 845 pence a share offer, Venture's management continued to insist that the Centrica offer undervalued the company.

Unusually for a hostile takeover, Venture's executives – or at least those below the CEO level – were key attractions for Centrica. Venture was a successful start-up and the board and management were significant shareholders. The chief executive and chief financial officer, who together led the bid defence, were expected to retire along with the company's founders, but Centrica was keen to hold onto Venture's operating management.

An early, comprehensive planning exercise put Centrica in a good position to take control of the company and move quickly on the integration. Consequently, when it became clear that shareholders' acceptance would reach the 75% threshold, Centrica had already set up a senior integration team and brought in an external team of advisers to help with the integration.

Early planning combined with good communication helped Centrica to tie down one of its target's most important assets: people. Centrica's advisory team developed a plan to approach Venture's staff with a clear and consistent message. At its core was a promise to Venture's highly entrepreneurial executive team that if they stayed on after the takeover, they stood an equal chance of being in charge of the merged business as those running Centrica's existing upstream gas division. The Venture team were impressed by the seniority of the people talking to them and the consistency of the messages.

Centrica was prepared to invest senior-management time into the initiative in addition to money spent on advisers. Soon after gaining control, Centrica's then CEO, Sam Laidlaw, and a director, Mark Hanafin, visited the Venture head office and had an informal meeting with the staff. There were two crucial parts to the message: the first was that they had an exciting vision for the combined business and they had bought Venture to enable that vision through their capabilities; the second was that Centrica had no preconceptions about how the merger would end up and Venture employees would be fully involved in the integration process. Hanafin then stayed all week, having meetings with Venture staff. Good communication cut both ways and the selection process for the new leadership team was rapid, transparent and fair. Any Centrica executives leaving as a result of the deal were treated with respect, and in fact stayed on to help with the integration.

As a result, just under 10% of Venture's employees left in the wake of the takeover and nearly all of these were back-office staff, made redundant because their functions were duplicated inside Centrica. Also crucial to retaining talent was the early decision to move the head office of the newly merged upstream business from Centrica's divisional headquarters in Windsor, near London, to Venture's headquarters in Aberdeen, Scotland, where many of Venture's staff worked and lived.

The move helped to define the culture of the new organisation. Centrica was aware of the cultural differences between an established FTSE 100 company and a start-up. There was a concern that the more formal and process-driven way of working at Centrica might stifle the capabilities it was seeking to acquire in Venture. But the Venture team, working with its new parent company, was actively encouraged to help design approval processes that would enable the newly combined organisation to operate better and more efficiently than previously. For example, new procedures ensured that the merged business – which was called Centrica Energy Upstream – could work with Centrica Group to make decisions about capital investment within three weeks of receiving a request, in line with Venture's practices before the acquisition. This was a visible demonstration that the entrepreneurial culture of Venture would be maintained under Centrica ownership.

The Centrica Energy Upstream integration was unusual because it was done without the business having a CEO; Jonathan Roger ultimately took up the role on completion of the integration. A senior integration team oversaw the integration, using a detailed milestone plan of just four months from the start of the merger to its completion. This was one month longer than the normal 100 days referred to in this book, but after the four months the new organisation could already operate on a business-as-usual basis. In that time the team consulted employees, moved head office, rebranded with a complete name change and introduced a new set of financial controls.

One of the deal's external advisers, David Overd, who worked on the integration, said:

> One of the most important factors was that we all knew what we were supposed to do by a given date and nobody wanted to be late. Nobody missed a deadline in the whole four-month period, which created a fantastic momentum.

Crucially, the integration also had the full commitment and support of Centrica's leadership team, which was involved from the outset in every aspect of the programme. But as well as having top-level buy-in, the integration plan delegated decision-making to the right levels, with a steering group directing individual project teams in areas such as IT and HR.

The focus during the integration was not on the cost-cutting redundancies, an integration strategy that in other deals often makes this phase more painful and difficult. Venture Production was instead an important strategic investment for Centrica, and at the heart of its strategy at that time to secure greater energy supplies to meet growing consumer demand.

Getting it wrong: the Zain way

Not everybody gets it right, however, and even the best business concepts can fail because of poor integration. The idea behind the expansion of Zain, formerly MTC Group, was better than average; in fact it was extremely good.

In a nutshell, Zain and its chief executive, Saad Al-Barrak – affectionately known by his staff as "Dr Saad" or, more simply, "The Doc" – realised what any student of the colonial history of North Africa and the Middle East knows: that many of the post-colonial national borders established in the wake of the first world war are wholly artificial.

For Saad, this simple concept inspired his approach to telecommunications consolidation in the region. In the first decade of the 21st century, Africa – and to some extent the Middle East – was making a giant leap in telecommunications, bypassing fixed-line telephony, which was expensive to install and rare, and taking customers straight to mobile.

Thus, although sub-Saharan Africa remained at the periphery of global markets, it was growing fast, with GDP increasing by 6% per year thanks to growing global demand for natural resources and, with it, rising commodities prices. Indeed, with 800 million people, it was the fastest-growing market in the mobile telecoms industry, with the lowest telecoms penetration rate in the world.

Many Africans, including those in nomadic tribes, regularly crossed national boundaries taking their mobile phones with them, especially in sub-Saharan Africa. Cheap Chinese handsets combined with cost-cutting at global companies such as Motorola and Philips were opening up the market. By the time Saad came along, it was ripe for exploitation.

Saad had helped MTC grow from a single-country mobile telecoms business in Kuwait to a regional Middle Eastern business with operations in Bahrain, Lebanon and Jordan. In 2005, Saad was thinking about further expansion into Africa, the hot new market for telecoms. Meanwhile, one of the continent's biggest operators, Celtel, was run by his friend Mohammed "Mo" Ibrahim, who had a group of committed investors including International Finance Corporation (IFC) and Actis Capital, an arm of the UK's international aid agency.

Celtel was the largest pan-African wireless service provider with forecast revenues of $1 billion for 2005 and a bright future. As Ibrahim put it:

> *Everyone thinks Africa is full of starving people and pretty lions. They don't realise that it is also full of normal people who want to make a telephone call.*

One $3.4 billion merger later (in March 2005), MTC was the owner of Celtel.

For two years MTC adopted a hands-off approach to the Celtel operations: the business benefited from MTC's access to and reputation in the financial markets, but there was little by way of integration. With little pan-African competition, Celtel, which at the point of its acquisition had operations in 11 countries, continued to perform well. MTC helped to fund its further expansion into Madagascar, Sudan and Nigeria.

However, by 2007 the situation was changing as aggressive new entrants from Asia and the Middle East began to compete to transform the mobile telecoms market. With this increased competition came increased expansion costs. For example, when MTC made its investment in Celtel, it paid the equivalent of $950 per mobile-phone subscriber, but less than a year later, when it bought the 61% of Sudan's Mobitel that it did not already own, it needed to pay $1,100 per subscriber.

MTC tried a number of special offers to increase its market share, including the introduction of a top-up service that allowed customers to top up credit at major supermarket chains using cash, critical in a region where many potential customers do not have credit cards. Its central differentiating strategy, however, was One Network, which provided regional tariffs without roaming charges. The service, launched in 2006, was the world's first borderless mobile-phone network, allowing 160 million people in six countries across east, west and central Africa to make calls without roaming surcharges. The technology behind the service was relatively simple. More difficult were the required regulatory approvals.

Then came a rebrand, in which the entire Middle Eastern/African network became Zain, which means beautiful or wonderful in Arabic. Saad's ambition was to make the brand one of the world's biggest: a name that could stand alongside Coca-Cola or Microsoft. He was not daunted by the fact that no telecoms operator had yet managed to achieve such brand recognition. Zain continued to expand, rolling out the One Network and buying more assets in Nigeria – a crucially large African country – back closer to home in Saudi Arabia and then finally, in 2009, in Morocco. By that point the group had operations in 24 countries across the region. However, the acquisitions had been made at lightning speed with no apparent overall plan and – despite headline-grabbers such as the company rebranding and the One Network concept – by 2010 there had still been little by way of group integration. Partly as a consequence of poor management and partly because competition in Africa continued to grow, Zain's African operations accounted for approximately 62% of its customers but only 15% of its net profit, according to the *Financial Times*.

With the large networks in Kenya and Nigeria in particular underperforming and the core group facing liquidity problems, the Al-Kharafi family (its major shareholder) became concerned and began to discuss the disposal of the African network. Saad resigned and was replaced as chief executive by Nabil bin Salama, who, later that year, sold almost all Zain's African assets to India's Bharti Airtel for $10.7 billion.

Zain refocused on its core Arab market and went on to make a successful push into Iraq, where in 2012 it had more than half of the market. The *Financial Times* described the company as "the model for the pruned [telecommunications] industry in 2012". That was probably not the legacy that Saad had wanted to have.

The 100-day post-closing period is crucial for the success or failure of a deal in the medium and long term. But it is important not to take a myopic approach to this truncated period. A good acquirer will bring skills and intelligence gleaned in the deal strategy and will know that integration does not end on day 100. The integration plan should make sure that the newly combined organisation becomes business as usual as rapidly as possible.

What is the litmus test of success in integration? When the employees stop talking nostalgically about the legacy companies.

When integration is finally complete, there will hopefully be both relief and pleasure that it is over. Sebastian James, following the merger of electronics retailers Carphone Warehouse and Dixons in 2014, told *Management Today* that during the process:

> We were worried it could all turn a bit Game of Thrones – you know, swords through the head type problems. But no. We've moved into our boyfriend's flat, we're off the honeymoon period now and have decided who puts the bins out and who does the washing up – the tasks are allocated.

To achieve this, it is impossible to overstate the importance of an early focus on time and resources in this phase of the deal. Where integration is not done comprehensively and effectively, the result can be the one discussed in the next chapter: corporate divorce.

Doing the deal right: dos and don'ts

- **Do** walk away where there are clear signs that you should not do the deal, or that it is starting to unravel.
- **Don't** hang on because you have put so much emotional – or real – currency into the deal: it is braver to walk away than cling on.
- **Don't** underestimate the potential cultural challenges of a merger.
- **Don't** forget that people are the most important business asset.
- **Do** be clear up front about which executives will get senior positions in the merged business.
- **Don't** forget that you must keep running the current business while at the same time integrating the new.
- **Do** take pain early – when you have difficult news to impart it does not get easier as time goes on.

- **Don't** throw away your due diligence, as it will be critical for developing your 100-day plan.

- **Don't** forget the need to get the target's employees onside early – or at least be as honest with them as possible. This will benefit the new owner.

- **Don't** stop integrating after 100 days, as a thorough merger could take years.

9

A most amicable divorce

EVEN THE BEST CORPORATE RELATIONSHIP does not always last forever. In this chapter, we have come full circle from corporate strategy, target selection and execution to divestments and spin-offs, some of the strategic alternatives to purchases considered earlier in this book.

Mistakes in doing a deal are not the only causes of corporate divorce. Sometimes a corporate relationship that was right in the past is so no longer, as the parent or the subsidiary or both change their strategy, the market conditions alter significantly, or technological disruption drives fundamental changes in the industry.

There are, however, many instances where an acquisition was flawed for one reason or another and subsequently needs to be resold. There are even some where the parent has made a series of mistakes over a longer period and ultimately has little choice but to split the company in two.

Breaking up is, as they say, hard to do. This can be the case whether the demerger is done by a full sale to a new owner or by a spin-off through a separate public listing, effectively retaining the same owners under separate structures.

Once a split is inevitable, attention needs to be paid to issues such as governance, strategy and talent to ensure an amicable break-up, maximise the best possible sale price and ensure the continued business of the two companies. This can work well where the acquisition was a fundamentally good one and it is then sold for a substantial profit, as in the case of Mergermarket Group (see below).

Why split up?

The decision to divest a business need not mean that the original decision to buy it was wrong. Companies often make acquisitions that subsequently turn to divested assets. A study by Donald Bergh, a professor at Daniels College of Business, University of Denver, in 1997 showed that acquisitions of unrelated or non-core assets have little more than a 50/50 chance of being retained five years after acquisition.

This continues today. Following a quiet period of activity during the financial crisis, divestments began to rise again. As the overall M&A market continues to rise, that trend is expected to continue.

A study by EY in 2015 based on 800 interviews with corporate executives of medium-sized to large companies found that 45% had recently divested a business or placed one on a watch-list. And 74% of the companies surveyed are using divestments, somewhat counter-intuitively, to help fund growth, as was the case with Diageo's early disposals (see Chapter 2).

The growth in shareholder activism is one of the most important drivers of this corporate behaviour for publicly listed companies, as the activists pressurise company boards to make hard strategic choices at a time of persistent slow economic growth or unclear strategic direction. Of these companies surveyed by EY, 16% said that shareholder activism was the most important trigger for their last divestment, and another 45% said it was a major consideration (see Figure 9.1).

A business or division's non-core or weak competitive position will lead to probable divestment, whether pressured by activists or a company's own internal strategic reviews. As in the case of CKI and UK Power Networks (see Chapter 3), many companies go through a continuous cycle of defining core operations and will look to sell divisions to raise cash and free up management resources to focus on operations closer to that core.

However, companies are also increasingly willing to divest for opportunistic reasons. According to the EY survey, 47% said that they would consider selling at a premium of 10–20% were they to get an unsolicited bid. As an acquirer, it pays to be alert for available assets, even if the owner has not put up a for sale sign. This relates to the need to develop a long list of potential targets.

FIGURE 9.1 **What drives divestments?**

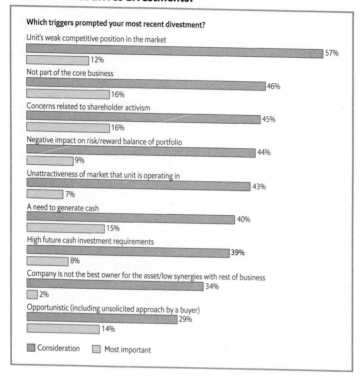

Which triggers prompted your most recent divestment?

Unit's weak competitive position in the market
57%
12%

Not part of the core business
46%
16%

Concerns related to shareholder activism
45%
16%

Negative impact on risk/reward balance of portfolio
44%
9%

Unattractiveness of market that unit is operating in
43%
7%

A need to generate cash
40%
15%

High future cash investment requirements
39%
8%

Company is not the best owner for the asset/low synergies with rest of business
34%
2%

Opportunistic (including unsolicited approach by a buyer)
29%
14%

■ Consideration   ■ Most important

Source: *Global Corporate Divestment Study*, EY, 2015

Global macroeconomic factors are an important driver of divestment deals. Many of the world's biggest companies are seeking to rebalance their portfolios towards emerging markets, as seen earlier with Diageo. The status quo has fundamentally changed. As companies realise this and rush to jump on the bandwagon, they will continue to divest their lower-growth divisions based in the developed world.

The EY study revealed one further point: when economic growth is heading upwards and valuations are increasing, the need for speed and getting the deal done seems to have risen to the top of the M&A agenda. Half of the companies surveyed said that the imperative to close deals quickly and with certainty was more important than waiting longer to secure a higher price.

HP: the 15-year road to divorce

As discussed above, there are many reasons for mergers not to survive in the medium to long term and by no means all of them signify that the acquisition was flawed. However, some companies are forced into disposals, demergers or spin-offs because they have a poor track record of buying and integrating businesses.

One such company is HP. This once-great company's merger with Compaq was probably ill-advised; but the takeover of UK-listed Autonomy was simply a disaster (as discussed in earlier chapters).

In mid-2014, under pressure from its investors, the company announced that it would split into two publicly traded units: Hewlett-Packard Enterprise and HP Inc, the former a more forward-looking business selling servers, software, networking and associated services and the latter the more traditional part of the business selling printers and personal computers – thus including a large portion of what was Compaq. In November 2015 the split took effect.

There has been much debate about exactly what went wrong for HP, but the Compaq purchase in 2001 seems to have started the decline. HP itself was built on acquisitions, with the first taking place back in 1958 and then accelerating in the 1990s and into the new millennium: between 1989 and 2015 it made 125 acquisitions.

In the wake of the Compaq acquisition, HP embarked on a series of large deals, each one seemingly worse than the last, culminating in the Autonomy debacle. Before HP was forced to write off $8.8 billion of the $11.1 billion purchase price of Autonomy in 2011, it took an $8 billion write-down on its 2008 acquisition of EDS, a computer services business for which it paid $13.9 billion. Before Leo Apotheker, the CEO in charge during the Autonomy deal, was fired, he had proposed a plan to sell off HP's PC division, but it was abandoned by his successor, Meg Whitman, when she took charge. Whitman finally threw in the towel and backed the demerger in 2014. In 2015, 16 years after the initial merger, HP Compaq formally split into two separate companies.

For all its difficulties, HP did take time to execute carefully an incredibly complicated demerger. Formal paperwork for the deal was filed in 2014, 18 months before the split, and the companies began to operate as two businesses for internal purposes six months before the demerger was formalised.

The financial terms of the split also seemed sensible, with the supposedly higher-growth Hewlett-Packard Enterprise shouldering the costs of its own restructuring, rather than heaping losses on the legacy printer and PC business. In a move that will at least provide board continuity, Whitman was made CEO of Hewlett-Packard Enterprise as well as chair of HP Inc.

The spin-off dumping ground

Spin-offs can be an effective way of separating assets with fundamentally different characteristics, allowing the stockmarket to price the growth prospects of each segment more accurately. However, the financial and strategic rationale of spin-offs is not always so clear; some deals use the spun-off company as a dumping ground for either liabilities or less attractive assets that cannot be sold.

One example is the 2013 split of Rupert Murdoch's US-listed media company, News Corporation, into a traditional print newspaper arm, which includes the *Wall Street Journal* and the *Times*, and 21st Century Fox, which owns the eponymous film studio, Fox News and a stake in BSkyB. The decision to split was made in the wake of a phone-hacking scandal, during which Murdoch closed his UK-based newspaper, the *News of the World*, but failed to avoid a wider shareholder revolt from investors with no interest in the other print-media assets.

In this case, however, Murdoch left his print empire with around $2.6 billion in cash with no debt, plus some legacy Australian TV assets that were still profitable and thus able to offset the continuing losses at the newspapers. The split seems to have worked: 21st Century Fox's share price has soared, while News Corporation's has fluctuated but not fallen more than 25% below the issue price. In today's world of online news delivery, this is a victory for an old-media company.

A less edifying example is Viacom's flotation of its video-rental chain Blockbuster. Unable to sell the company, Viacom spun it off in 1999, but just before doing so arranged for it to borrow $1 billion to cover a final special dividend of $905 million. Blockbuster was soon overwhelmed by massive changes in the media industry as the internet developed. After many years of struggling, it filed for bankruptcy in 2010.

Another way of offloading undesired assets is to pay someone to take them off your hands. This was the route followed by UK-listed Anglo-French retailer Kesa when disposing of its troubled electrical retail arm, Comet. To sweeten the sale, Kesa left Comet with a £50 million ($80 million) dowry, as well as retaining responsibility for its employee pension liabilities. The business was sold to OpCapita, the investment vehicle of US financier Henry Jackson, for £2. Yet less than two years later it collapsed, owing the UK government nearly £70 million in tax and statutory redundancy payments. OpCapita banked £100 million from the deal, leaving the government fuming, but ultimately unwilling to take legal action.

Getting divestment decisions right

In making and executing decisions to invest and divest, companies should follow four basic rules.

1 Have the right information to manage a portfolio successfully

Frequent portfolio reviews enable companies to react quickly to changes in the market and reallocate capital accordingly; by doing this, non-core businesses can also be sold at the optimal time. However, 58% of the executives of the companies surveyed by EY in 2015 acknowledged that they do not go through this process frequently enough. Best practice would suggest that a review should be done every six months, if not more frequently. This applies to both large and small companies, although larger, older companies are more likely to have amassed a greater number of now non-core businesses than newer ones. But that does not mean that every company of any size should not continuously assess what could be spun off. They should.

To complete such a review, companies must understand the way costs are allocated to different business units, use the right industry benchmarks and develop tailored analytical tools to make sense of any available big data. As part of this process, medium and large companies should improve communication between the board and the in-house or external M&A team and their shareholders.

2 Learn value-creation lessons from private equity

Private equity firms can be masters of value creation at sale. The key to this is planning: prepare for a sale early. If the company has 12–24 months to prepare, the business being divested should be treated internally as a stand-alone entity as soon as possible. There may also be time to be creative, for instance by expanding into different geographies or markets using a joint-venture agreement, although beware of the pitfalls discussed in Chapter 1. Extracting working capital, which buyers tend not to pay more for, is an easy-to-achieve option. If the company has less than 12 months to prepare, at least establish a clear story of how the asset might be attractive to prospective buyers.

3 Improve divestment execution

Again, planning is crucial. EY's study found that high-performing companies are 50% more likely to have begun their sale preparation at a much earlier stage than low-performers, which start late and therefore have to take short cuts.

It is essential to put in place the right governance structure for a sale, probably with an executive steering committee that can make quick decisions. The specific asset(s) for sale should also be rigorously defined, but this specification should allow for different sales options for potential buyers who may not want all parts of the business.

IT can often be the most complex area of any organisation or division to be sold, so this will usually require the longest lead-time. The tax structure of a divestment should also be optimised (yet kept flexible as the final tax structure is dependent on the buyer). Lastly, the sale should be analysed from the perspective of different types of buyers, both trade and private equity, to create the best possible sales pitch.

4 Strike the right balance between speed and value

The ideal solution is to prepare the sale over a long period, but that assumes flexibility on timing that many companies do not have. There may be significant pressures on timing because deal uncertainty could damage an asset, the window of opportunity to sell may be narrow, or the capital may be needed urgently to invest elsewhere.

However, to maximise value, a seller should invest – and not underinvest, as will be the temptation – during the sale-preparation period to create additional value for the asset and to attract additional buyers. Try to put yourself in the buyer's position to understand better what story will sell most strongly, including the potential synergies for each type of buyer.

Mergermarket Group: from start-up to global player

The business life cycle of Mergermarket Group, a financial news and data provider, since 2000 shows that there are times when it is beneficial to be part of a large corporation and times when it is better to be a stand-alone company.

Mergermarket had a modest start at an inauspicious time. Born in 2000 in the wake of the dotcom bust, it was the brainchild of Caspar Hobbs, a former army major, and Charlie Welsh, a journalist at *Financial News*, a UK-based publication.

At the core of the business was its subscription-revenue model, a system that the world's biggest newspapers are still struggling to push through a decade and half later. The service mixed timely and proprietary intelligence from and about expected and completed corporate events (M&A deals, IPOs and other capital-raising activities) with good data from external sources. It found its feet with the almost universal adoption among bankers and other advisers of the BlackBerry, which allowed them to receive instant intelligence direct to their mobile phone wherever they were.

By 2005, Mergermarket's revenues were £18 million ($34 million), sufficient to give the early-stage investors an exit. The business was sold to Pearson, a UK-listed media company and owner of the *Financial Times*, for £101 million ($192 million).

At the time Pearson was headed by Marjorie Scardino, who famously promised that Pearson would sell its crown jewel asset, the *Financial Times*, only "over her dead body". The chief executive of the Financial Times Group was Rona Fairhead, who saw in Mergermarket a business that had already mastered the digital environment at a time when the *FT*'s online service, FT.com, was young, free to use and loss-making.

Hamilton Matthews, CEO of Mergermarket, had been brought in in 2001 from the capital markets division of Thomson Financial to run the commercial side of the operation; by 2009 he was running the business. Matthews says:

> *We didn't have to go through the digital integration legacy issues, which was why the FT wanted us so much. When newspaper sponsorship started to fall, it suddenly became a very hard model to make work.*

Explaining the rationale for the deal, Fairhead said that Mergermarket would add "proprietary content, a premium customer base, reliable growth from new revenue sources and attractive financial characteristics" to the FT Group. Fairhead also highlighted opportunities to develop new products jointly, increase advertising and sponsorship revenues, and share IT with other parts of the FT Group.

However, the FT Group took advantage of only one of those potential factors, the attractive financial characteristics of Mergermarket, which enabled Pearson to reap more than three times its purchase price when it sold the business seven years later.

The terms of the acquisition included a two-year earn-out that prevented any meaningful integration during that period, meaning Mergermarket was left alone to concentrate on its globalisation strategy. But even after that, the businesses were kept almost completely separate, with no integration of customers and IT and few joint-product launches. Notably, *Financial Times* journalists covering the capital markets used and quoted data from a competitor, Dealogic, rather than their in-house source, Mergermarket.

Nevertheless, for Mergermarket the tie-up was helpful, Matthews claimed:

> It was great for us to join such a credible media organisation and it
> made it much easier for the editorial team to be able to get leads and
> sources once we were part of the FT.

He added:

> But any form of integration cannot be forced because it won't work
> and the argument was that the brands and the culture were very
> different, both on the sales and on the editorial side. But some of it was
> madness, such as people who wanted to join us from the FT – or vice
> versa – having to interview in the open market.

Later, even though Fairhead tried to get the five divisional CEOs
of the FT Group to collaborate on smaller projects, there was still
no real integration. When the financial crisis hit in 2008, the group
moved into defensive mode and the individual CEOs prioritised their
own businesses. As time went on, Pearson shifted its focus further
towards the education sector, and when Scardino was replaced as chief
executive by John Fallon, the group made clear that its future focus
would be 100% on that area.

As a result, Mergermarket was put on the block in 2013. It was sold
to a private equity firm, BC Partners, for £382 million ($608 million),
which was used to fund the initial losses incurred on setting up FT.com
and in the long run helped turn that business into a profitable venture,
with over 500,000 paying subscribers in 2015.

Subsequently, Pearson sold both the Financial Times Group and its
investment in The Economist Group (publisher of *The Economist*), long
regarded as the jewels in its corporate crown.

Meanwhile, Mergermarket was finding that life was very different
with BC Partners. Matthews says:

> We loved being part of Pearson for seven years. It was the right home
> for us, but we were crying out for investment. We are an innovative
> business – we wanted to be able to make acquisitions, launch new
> products and do it quickly.

BC Partners, which already used Mergermarket's products, knew the
business well by the time it bought it. The first thing it did was help
Matthews to transform Mergermarket's technology platform, bringing

in a new chief technical officer it had worked with in another portfolio company and building a new 45-person IT team.

The plan – an IT consolidation initiative together with a number of focused acquisitions – was to double pre-tax profits from the level they were at the time of the purchase. By 2015, Mergermarket had grown to include over 1,000 staff, including 500 editors, researchers and analysts, each expert in that niche financial market.

The investor's view

At 30 years old, BC Partners is one of the most venerable private equity firms, managing assets worth over €12 billion ($17 billion) globally. Where some rivals have eschewed the media sector, particularly publishing, BC Partners has been prepared to take a punt on the right business, also buying Springer, a German science and business publisher, in 2013.

So when Pearson put Mergermarket up for auction, BC Partners was at the front of the queue. Managing partner Nikos Stathopoulos explains:

> A combination of reasons attracted us. First of all, it is the market leader in a highly attractive and fast-growing segment of the market, it is diversified and revenue-generative and the space is highly fragmented so we could see opportunities for both organic growth and acquisitions.

With all the usual private equity investment drivers ticked, BC Partners drilled down during the due diligence process and found strong management, a subscription business model that allowed Mergermarket to get paid in advance for the year and renewal rates of 90%.

Did BC Partners have any doubts about taking on journalists, a section of the populace most in private equity go out of their way to avoid? Stathopoulos says:

> As an investor you always have some concern when the assets go home every night. What gave us comfort here is that you have a market leader who we feel historically has managed to recruit and retain its

staff because of a combination of the company's growth prospects, pay or conditions.

We also looked at Mergermarket's pre-publication verification process and its accuracy and were highly comforted by the company's very low record of editorial complaints.

The breadth and depth of Mergermarket's talent pool across editorial, research and data analysis was seen by BC Partners to be a competitive advantage and a significant barrier to entry, as having such scale and reach is hard to replicate, but it also means no one individual is indispensable to the business.

After taking over, BC Partners took a four-pronged approach to growing Mergermarket, which included having no significant losses of personnel, investing cash in IT infrastructure, funding acquisitions for Mergermarket to expand its products and services, and finally – and perhaps most importantly for what was already a successful people business – leaving Mergermarket's employee culture and environment virtually intact.

On this last point, Mergermarket journalists are allowed to write independently about investments related to BC Partners. In line with its private equity mantra of incentivising performance by linking it to pay, BC Partners realigned the packages of sales staff. It also introduced a management equity scheme that includes not just the executive board of the company but also the second tier of management, so all the key executives have private equity's desired "skin in the game". The scheme is believed to be one of the broadest in place at a private equity-owned business.

For many financial buyers, corporate spin-offs are low-hanging fruit. Noting that in its last full financial year (2012) under Pearson, Mergermarket's turnover of $100 million equated to only around 1.5% of the parent group's revenue so was clearly non-core, Stathopoulos says:

We feel that spin-offs have been broadly successful investments mainly when they involve small divisions of large corporates where they tend to be under-invested and under-focused. Once they become stand-alone, the management is better motivated and focused to grow and the owners to invest. This is especially true with a fast-growing business like Mergermarket.

When the time is right, Mergermarket will be sold through a trade sale or to another private equity investor, or be listed via an IPO. If it is the former, will Mergermarket find a more permanent home inside a big corporation the second time around? The answer, thinks Stathopoulos, may be "yes". A more mature business, he feels, might benefit from adding a fast-growing, diversified global business. It would offer synergies, while not needing the same level of hands-on attention and investment that had been required during Mergermarket's high-growth phase in the period immediately following its purchase by BC Partners in 2013.

This case also demonstrates what can be done in M&A by financial sponsor firms, such as those doing private equity, whose business it is to buy and sell companies. This is directly related to the principal focus of this chapter – amicable corporate divorces – because selling all their acquisitions is the goal of these firms.

These expert acquirers have shifted their business models over the years, and clearly recognise the necessity to focus on the big three issues that have been discussed throughout this book: planning, communication and people. Indeed, the global co-head of private equity at White & Case, Ian Bagshaw, explained it as follows:

Over-leverage has historically been the key cause of PE [private equity] deal failure with the focus on servicing debt and ultimately managing creditors. But now it's a case of "back to the future" as the key challenge is ensuring that the executive team is right and that they are hitting the plan, which can often involve a series of bolt-on acquisitions through the investment period. As the private equity industry has developed and moved away from financial engineered returns to focus again on growth as a primary driver of buy-out returns, the need for a team to run the business and execute synergy extraction through an executed build-out has never been higher.

PE deal doing is ultimately about backing the right people and therefore the biggest issue is whether you have them in the team.

In summary, as the Mergermarket deal demonstrates, breaking up is not necessarily a bad thing to do. Indeed, with the right attention, investment and planning, once-unloved assets can be polished up into real gems. However, for buyers and sellers alike, the foundation is in the planning and making sure that a sale or an acquisition fits with the company's strategy. And if staff or the incumbent management are crucial to that business, that includes keeping them onside too.

A most amicable divorce: dos and don'ts

- **Do** keep it friendly. Make sure management remains on good terms during a split; you might get less money for a sale without them.

- **Do** remember that, if you are a buyer, corporate carve-outs have a track record of being good bargains.

- **Do** take a lesson on value creation from private equity. Go for a high-growth business if the acquisition is central to your strategy – at least you will be able to sell it on for a profit later, if necessary.

- **Don't** become complacent in your approach to your business portfolio. Evaluate market conditions for selling assets or subsidiaries continually and formally, at least every six months.

- **Do** expedite the sale process – the market hates uncertainty.

- **Do** act before an activist investor joins your shareholder register and forces you to take action.

- **Don't** procrastinate in your sales preparation process. Start 12–18 months before a sale if possible, focusing on operational and financial housecleaning and on crystallising the value proposition for key buyers.

Conclusion: hunting the corporate yeti

M&A IS HERE to stay.

As the global economy continues to grow and businesses push to expand and integrate across national boundaries, the long-term trend is for more and more mergers, whatever the cyclical hiccups along the way. This is true whether the companies are large or small, or in high-tech or traditional industries. However, as discussed in the introductory chapters, numerous studies have found that in the longer term mergers and acquisitions destroy value in more than half of deals, even if the overall contribution of those deals to both companies and the economy overall is positive.

Many of these studies have also found that successful buyers can add huge financial value for their shareholders in both the short and long term if the deals are done well. But too many failed deals still occur – which is surprising given that the reasons for failure, as discussed throughout this book, are often public and clearly visible to other dealmakers.

The M&A equation should be simple: well-run and well-managed companies can execute good acquisition strategies with an overall financial benefit for their shareholders and the wider economy.

Disappointingly, although more and more acquisitions are being made, there is little evidence that since the turn of the millennium companies are getting better at them. The success rate is much better than during the 1980s and 1990s, when the failure rate was as much as 70–80%, according to some studies. But the 50/50 success rate achieved in the early 2000s has not been improved upon. And that is still no better than a flip of the coin.

We are currently operating in a very different environment. During the recent merger booms, the consequences of bad decision-making were magnified when the markets turned. You need only look at some of the pre-financial crisis deals outlined in this book to be concerned that history will repeat itself if lessons are not learnt. Bad deals do not necessarily manifest themselves as such until the good times stop. Thus some of the deals being done that look excellent now may well turn into failures later.

We have set out a simple, easy-to-follow set of rules that will help companies avoid the obvious mistakes that sink so many deals. We hope in doing so to champion a more rigorous and thoughtful approach to M&A that will benefit the wider economy at the macro level. If this is too ambitious a goal, we hope at least that these ideas will help you to make your company, at the micro level, one of the winners at merging with and acquiring other companies.

Throughout this book we have tried to distil our thoughts to useable, practical nuggets. In an attempt to concentrate our mantra, here are our final five recommendations:

- **Don't** treat M&A as a strategy: it is only a tactic to achieving a company's long-term goals. As outlined in Chapters 1 and 2, M&A is not the only method through which you can achieve long-term goals. Consider the others first, but once you have decided on M&A you will need to dedicate significant time, money and management resources to executing the deal.

- **Do** remember that M&A dealmaking is an art, not a science. At the same time, remember that M&A deals involve emotions and pressure for the CEO and the board to perform, and this percolates throughout the organisation once the deal is announced. As seen in Chapters 5, 6 and 7, executives who see the main chance and are agile enough to reach it, who can listen and negotiate, and who are focused but still flexible will carry the day. They will also realise that sometimes carrying the day means walking away from a broken deal.

- **Don't** focus only on doing the right deal, as doing the deal right is equally important. This is perhaps the most important lesson. As set out in Chapters 2, 3 and 4, doing the groundwork of good target selection, extensive due diligence and careful pricing will provide you with the right foundations for this. The practices outlined in Chapter 8 will then help you to integrate your acquisition. Remember that it is only at this post-closing stage that you will reap the benefits of all your hard work. Post-deal implementation attracts less attention and scrutiny than the pre-deal period, but it is where the real value can be added or destroyed irrespective of the rationale of the deal. Having the perfect business and synergy case but with flawed execution will not yield success.

- **Don't** make the same mistakes twice: make sure to do a post-audit review of each deal whether successful or not, so that you can learn for the next time. Even legendary serial dealmakers such as General Electric in the 1980s and 1990s and Cisco Systems in the first decade of this millennium get it wrong sometimes. The difference is that they learn from their mistakes, and when they do it again they have a better chance to do it right. Having a thorough and objective understanding of what went well or badly at each stage of the deal is crucial to avoid falling into the same pitfalls next time. Creating a corporate knowledge base that is actively applied by and institutionalised within the company as a whole (rather than being only in the heads of a few executives) is a critical component of successful dealmaking. If things do go wrong, cut your losses and remember our guidelines for a good divorce in Chapter 9.

- **Don't** forget the three big mistakes of dealmaking – planning, communication and people. As we have shown throughout this book, companies that make mistakes in these areas fail. The soft stuff is the hard stuff. You might be lucky and get away with one or two deals, but if you do any more than that, like HP in many of its acquisitions but especially its disastrous purchase of Autonomy, you will fail.

And finally, we would like to leave you with a challenge. As authors and practitioners, we have been unable to a find a deal where more than one of the big three mistakes were made and the acquirers subsequently managed to bring it back from the brink of disaster. The reason we wrote this book is because we believe the best way to learn is from mistakes: our own and those of others. So we invite you to hunt with us for the

"M&A yeti" – the worst deal to come back from the brink. Readers are asked to submit ideas to our microsite blog: whydealsfail.org.

Acknowledgements

WE ARE INDEBTED to a number of people in producing the research for this book. Helen Power, together with editor Clare Grist Taylor at Profile Books, has been integral in making sure our thoughts on this topic are coherently and correctly reflected on paper. We want to thank them for their efforts and accept that any remaining errors are our own. Michel and Anna are also thankful to EY LLP for support while allowing their editorial freedom. The research we have referred to in this book would not have been possible without the help of Naaguesh Appadu, Daniel King, Nikolay Vasilyev and Valeriya Vitkova – currently or previously of Cass Business School – and Philip Whitchelo of Intralinks. Finally, we are grateful for our families' understanding when we have had to spend time on this book instead of them.

Further reading

Angwin, Duncan (ed.), *Mergers and Acquisitions*, Blackwell Publishing, 2007.

Arzac, Enrique R., *Valuation for Mergers, Buy-outs, and Restructuring*, 2nd edition, John Wiley & Sons, 2008.

Bragg, Steven M., *Mergers & Acquisitions: A Condensed Practitioners' Guide*, John Wiley & Sons, 2009.

Bruner, Robert F., *Applied Mergers & Acquisitions*, University Edition, Wiley, 2004.

Bruner, Robert F., *Deals From Hell: M&A Lessons that Rise above the Ashes*, John Wiley & Sons, 2005.

Cadbury, Deborah, *Chocolate Wars – From Cadbury to Kraft: 200 Years of Sweet Success and Bitter Rivalry*, Harper Press, 2010.

Clark, Peter J. & Mills, Roger W., *Masterminding the Deal: Breakthroughs in M&A Strategy & Analysis*, Kogan Page, 2013.

Clemente, Mark N. and Greenspan, David S., *Winning at Mergers and Acquisitions: The Guide to Market-Focused Planning and Integration*, John Wiley & Sons, 1998.

Davidoff, Steven M., *Gods at War: Shotgun Takeovers, Government by Deal, and the Private Equity Implosion*, John Wiley & Sons, 2009.

Davis, Danny A., *M&A Integration – How To Do It: Planning and Delivering M&A Integration for Business Success*, John Wiley & Sons, 2012.

DePamphilis, Donald M., *Mergers, Acquisitions, and Other Restructuring Activities*, 8th Edition, Academic Press, 2015.

Evans, Frank C. and Bishop, David M., *Valuation for M&A Building Value in Private Companies*, John Wiley & Sons, 2001.

Faulkner, David, Teerikangas, Satu and Joseph, Richard J. (eds), *The Handbook of Mergers and Acquisitions*, Oxford University Press, 2012.

Galpin, Timothy J. and Herndon, Mark, *The Complete Guide to Mergers and Acquisitions: Process Tools to Support M&A Integration at Every Level*, Jossey Bass, 2000.

Gaughan, Patrick A., *Mergers, Acquisitions, and Corporate Restructurings*, 5th edition, John Wiley & Sons, 2010.

Hoffman, Norman W., *Mergers and Acquisitions Strategy for Consolidations: Roll Up, Roll Out, and Innovate for Superior Growth and Returns*, McGraw Hill, 2012.

Koller, Goedhart and Wessels, *Valuation: Measuring and Managing The Value of Companies*, Wiley Finance, 2010.

Moeller, Scott, *Surviving M&A: Make the Most of Your Company Being Acquired*, John Wiley & Sons, 2009.

Moeller, Scott (ed.), *The M&A Collection: Themes in Best Practice*, Bloomsbury, 2014.

Moeller, Scott and Brady, Chris, *Intelligent M&A: Navigating the Mergers and Acquisitions Minefield*, 2nd Edition, John Wiley & Sons, 2014.

Rosenbaum, Pearl and Harris, *Investment Banking: Valuation, Leveraged Buy-outs, and Mergers and Acquisitions*, Wiley Finance, 2013.

Pettit, Barbara S. and Ferris, Kenneth R., *Valuation for Mergers and Acquisitions*, 2nd edition, Pearson Education, 2013.

Schmidlin, Nicolas, *The Art of Company Valuation and Financial Statement Analysis*, John Wiley & Sons, 2014.

Siegenthaler, Paul J., *Perfect M&As: The Art of Business Integration*, Ecademy Press, 2009.

Sudarsanam, Sudi, *Creating Value from Mergers and Acquisitions*, 2nd edition, Pearson, 2010.

Wasserstein, Bruce, *Big Deal 2000: The Battle for Control of America's Leading Corporations*, Warner Books, 2000.

Index

Page numbers in *italics* indicate figures; those in **bold** indicate tables.

PublicAffairs is a publishing house founded in 1997. It is a tribute to the standards, values, and flair of three persons who have served as mentors to countless reporters, writers, editors, and book people of all kinds, including me.

I. F. STONE, proprietor of *I. F. Stone's Weekly*, combined a commitment to the First Amendment with entrepreneurial zeal and reporting skill and became one of the great independent journalists in American history. At the age of eighty, Izzy published *The Trial of Socrates*, which was a national bestseller. He wrote the book after he taught himself ancient Greek.

BENJAMIN C. BRADLEE was for nearly thirty years the charismatic editorial leader of *The Washington Post*. It was Ben who gave the *Post* the range and courage to pursue such historic issues as Watergate. He supported his reporters with a tenacity that made them fearless and it is no accident that so many became authors of influential, best-selling books.

ROBERT L. BERNSTEIN, the chief executive of Random House for more than a quarter century, guided one of the nation's premier publishing houses. Bob was personally responsible for many books of political dissent and argument that challenged tyranny around the globe. He is also the founder and longtime chair of Human Rights Watch, one of the most respected human rights organizations in the world.

·　　·　　·

For fifty years, the banner of Public Affairs Press was carried by its owner Morris B. Schnapper, who published Gandhi, Nasser, Toynbee, Truman, and about 1,500 other authors. In 1983, Schnapper was described by *The Washington Post* as "a redoubtable gadfly." His legacy will endure in the books to come.

Peter Osnos, *Founder and Editor-at-Large*